STRONG
IS THE CURRENT

*A Grieving Father's Meditations
on Life, Loss and Fishing*

JOEL SPRING

Published by:
West River Media
P.O. Box 15
Grand Island, NY 14072

Printed in the United States of America

First Edition

10 9 8 7 6 5 4 3 2 1

Catalog-in-Publication Data is available on file.

ISBN 978-0-9633109-8-9

Library of Congress Control Number: 2018956104

DEDICATION

This book is for my daughters,
Jessica Taylor and Jennifer Spring.

Strong is the Current

Time is a sort of river of passing events, and strong is its current. No sooner is a thing brought to sight than it is swept by and another takes its place, and this too will be swept away.

— *Marcus Aurelius*

Table of Contents

The Partial Eclipse

The white spinnerbait clanked against the half-submerged branch in a tinkle of tin blades and the unmistakable thump of lead on wood. I let it sink for a moment before beginning the retrieve. Watching the murky water behind the lure for the telltale sign of something following, I was neither surprised nor disappointed when the spinnerbait reached the side of the kayak without so much as a follow from a curious bluegill. I'd hoped for a bass or a pike or even something more exotic such as a bowfin. Twenty some-odd casts into my post-work kayak launch into my home creek, I hadn't seen a thing.

I didn't yet want to break out the silly eclipse glasses in my dry-box. Still, the woodlands lining the creek, the water and the sky itself exhibited a subtle, curious color change. It wasn't precisely the warm light of dawn or sunset, nor was it the diffuse light of an overcast day. The sky was a brilliant blue, but the highlights of the trees and water were losing their yellows and reds. The blues and greens seemed to glow. My home water was becoming an alien landscape. I checked my watch. 2:30 p.m. It was nearly peak time for the 2017 eclipse. Not for the first time in my fishing life, I'd lost track of time and it was later than I thought. Reaching into the dry-box, I removed the cheap eclipse glasses that had been given out at work. I couldn't decide if it was a nice gesture from my company or an assumption that the employees weren't bright enough (a little eclipse humor) to know enough not to look directly at the sun during the eclipse. I suppose it was thoughtful either way. Laying the paddle across my lap and stowing the fishing rod, I removed my sunglasses. Holding the cardboard eclipse glasses to my face, I looked upward. The shadow of the moon began moving across the fiery face of the sun, looking like a dark inverse of the familiar crescent moon dressed in funereal black. Taking the glasses off, I resumed fishing. I'd check again in a few moments.

I switched out the white spinnerbait for a chartreuse one. With no method to my madness, I cast again into the tangled roots and branches lining the creek bank. When I was a kid, I caught a lot of bass, pike and bowfin on a chartreuse spinnerbait. As an adult, I caught more fish on a white spinnerbait. I couldn't decide which to use on eclipse day, so I switched back and forth several times. *Past, present, past, present.*

The natural sunlight dimmed even further and I guessed the eclipse had arrived at what would pass for peak at this latitude. Several hundred miles north of totality, we had to settle for a 71% eclipse. The strange colors of my home water became more vivid as the daylight faded in increments as much imagined as seen. I thought about grabbing the eclipse glasses but elected the fisherman's maxim of *just one more cast.*

Again the spinnerbait thumped against a thigh-thick branch. Before I could let it sink an inch, the line jerked violently sideways. I suspected a bowfin from the hard strike—and from that prehistoric beast's propensity for hanging out in downed trees. When it made a run for the surface, however, upon its first flip out of the water I recognized the dark greens and yellows of a largemouth bass. I wasn't disappointed, though I would rather it had been a bowfin. I have a soft spot for the ancient fishes and their tackle-destroying antics, but more on that later. I lipped the four-pound bass at the side of the kayak, and hauled him in to briefly admire and photograph. His colors and markings were striking, made strangely translucent in the growing semi-darkness. Supporting the bass underwater until he streaked away with a powerful flip of the tail, I figured there must be some kind of story to catching a fish in the midst of the eclipse, even if it's just a bass.

Putting the silly glasses back on, I watched the moon roll across the face of the sun for a few minutes. For a moment, I pointed my small camera at the sky, hoping for the best but not daring to look. A 71% solar eclipse is not high drama, though it's interesting and infrequent enough to draw a lot of attention. Watching the news the past few weeks to see how many people were drawn to the path of totality, I was surprised at the hype. Traffic jams, booked hotels. It became something of a celebration. I wonder how many of these eclipse travelers spent much time with other natural phenomenon such as, say, the small creek running through their town. As with anything promising to be even remotely exciting, the hype became almost unbearable. If I never hear the phrase *path of totality* again in my life, it will be too soon. But it was pleasant enough. It was just another distraction. For me, that's what fishing is all about lately.

One year ago to the day of the eclipse, I took my 23-year-old daughter on her last fishing trip. Jennifer was only three months away from succumbing to the merciless ravages of brain cancer. (Forget *path of totality*. If I never hear the words *brain cancer* ever again it will be too soon). She'd endured radical brain surgery, chemotherapy, radiation, infections and months and months of pain, confusion and heartache. That day on my nephew's boat on Canandaigua, one of New York's Finger Lakes, she was exhausted and nauseous and didn't make it more than a half-hour. Porter and I fished hard, desperately trying to hook a fish Jennifer could fight. The lake was uncharacteristically rough, full of gray sky and whitecaps. We were all buffeted in the boat, but Jen suffered most of all. She'd been given four to six months to live and would just make four. She wanted to fish, though, and she wanted a boat ride. Jennifer was long past being able to kayak fish with me. I figured that Porter's boat was the biggest, most stable option we had and, with his talent for finding lake trout, I thought we might even get her a big fish.

From somewhere down around 80 feet, according to Porter's fish finder, I felt a tug and a headshake. I set the hook with a vengeance and began reeling. It felt like a good fish. I handed the rod to Jen. She reeled, excited. In only a few seconds, the fish was off. She laughed. I'm glad she laughed.

"Dad, I hate to ask, but can we go back to the dock?"

She was so sick. Jennifer hadn't been fishing for herself. She wanted to fish one last time with me. We both knew it. My wife, Joy, daughter Jessica and Porter all knew it as well.

One year ago today.

The moon passed from the face of the sun and the reds and yellows returned to the landscape. A warm breeze blowing from the farm fields to the south signaled the return to everyday life.

If only.

My personal eclipse, nine months after my youngest daughter died in my arms, shows no sign of brightening. If I had to put a number on the totality of my emotional eclipse, I think 71% is as good a number as any. I've been operating on the remaining 29% of myself for nine months now. The colors have faded and I sometimes struggle to see life's bright corona around the edges of this dark eclipse. I've done what I can with that 29%, but most days it isn't enough. It's not enough for Joy, or for Jessica (who needs her dad more than ever), and on many days it isn't enough to even help me put one foot in front of the other without falling. I fall a lot these days. Some days the totality of my eclipse is much more than 71%, truth be told.

I've been fishing a lot, trying to outrun the darkness.

The creek was still now. A lone osprey patrolled high above, looking for his next meal. I watched him dive and tread water before coming up with something shiny and silver, probably a shad. Looking at the rods on the deck, I tried to decide what to do next. Folding the silly eclipse glasses in on themselves, I placed them in the small plastic dry box by my feet. The box holds the necessities like my keys, phone (it's usually off these days) and extra camera batteries. Being something of a superstitious sort, it also holds some magic tokens. At the bottom of the box is a dollar bill that I found floating near a yacht club several weeks earlier (it was the only catch of the day and, since it was near a yacht club, I would have hoped for something more like a $20 or even $100). On top of the dollar bill is Jennifer's last fishing license. And now, the eclipse glasses.

One year ago today.

I fished just a little longer, floating in the same creek where Jennifer used to fish with me. I fish to keep my sanity, such as it is. I also do it because, through all of her treatments and every afternoon that I spent at her bedside, Jen always wanted her friends and family to live their lives and not just spend every moment thinking about her. I also do it because she no longer can.

Pausing for a moment in my casting, I wondered about 2024. Eight years from now, a total solar eclipse is coming. This time we are in the *path of totality*. I wonder if the pain will be any easier by then. I think the answer is an easy and definitive *no*. I've read a lot on grief these past few months and one of the ideas that stuck with me is that you start grieving the day your child dies and stop grieving the day *you* die. It's only been nine months, but I believe this bit of wisdom is likely true.

I started casting again.

When I got home and uploaded the photos, the photo of the bass in the mute light of the partial eclipse was unremarkable. But something else gave me pause. Only one of the several eclipse photos I attempted through the silly glasses was in focus. In the frame, the eclipsed sun took on the shape of a heart. It didn't make sense, as the true partial eclipse would have looked (if anything) like an inverted heart. This one was just a heart. All through Jen's illness I hoped for a sign from God. Since then, my faith remains, though much more out of habit than devotion. The heart was vivid and orange. I choose to think it was a sign not from God, but from Jennifer.

Sitting at the computer that night with the flaming heart illuminating my monitor, the ideas for this book began to flow together. Like life, this book is a river with many sources. Some days the river carries me effortlessly along, giving me a temporary reprieve from the memories of death and the reality of my own despair as I cast for fish and drift further and further from the safety of the launch.

Other days, I have to paddle harder.

Rites of Spring

The very upper stretch of my creek runs conveniently through my backyard. Well, to be completely accurate, it runs through my *neighbor's* backyard. A small drainage feeds the main part of the creek and runs through (and occasionally up and over) my backyard. During years where the water levels are high enough, we see steelhead and, less commonly, salmon in our own little ditch. Where the ditch joins the creek, the creek still isn't much of a creek, so it's a treat to see those big eight-pound rainbows and twenty-pound salmon streaking up and down the anemic confines of the creek's upper limits. I have a habit, especially in the early spring, of walking down the road (all of fifty yards) to the bridge over the creek. It's not hard to tell when the steelhead have arrived. With only a minute or two of observation, splashing and silvery streaks will quickly acknowledge the fishes' presence, poorly hidden in the diminutive flow. I undertake these mini-scouting trips once or twice a day until I finally spot a fish in the current and then it's *game-on*.

With a winter spent sulking, grieving and generally making a depressing nuisance of myself to anyone within emotional shooting range, I started checking the creek in early March. Winter dragged on well into the month, as it always does in Western New York. One day after work, a March snow (the most unwelcome snow of all) put a fresh blanket on my entire neighborhood, including the upper banks of my creek. Nonetheless, I walked down to the bridge. To my amazement, two roostertails of spray shot up from the creek, not thirty yards from the bridge, as several large steelhead vied for position. Turning on my heels without a second glance, I hurried at a pace my neighbors might have considered a *run* but was, in actuality, more of a *trot*. Not much of a runner, I can trot with the best of them. I didn't need to search for my gear. It was all piled in the garage and ready to go and had been for months. The rod was rigged and ready. Boots and waders were ready. I trotted back down the road more slowly this time, only because I was wearing chest waders. I could only assume my neighbors were once again watching, rolling their eyes at me. Not many people fish *the ditch* and it always draws a few strange looks whenever I do.

I've fished this stretch since I was a kid. When I was that kid, I never really caught anything other than suckers. The spooky rainbows always saw me coming or were scared off down the creek with my splashy casting of whatever incorrect offering I happened to be throwing in their direction. I do recall catching several large salmon by physically pouncing on them. They're a bit more hapless than the rainbows. Many years ago, pheasant hunting in the fields not far from my home, I was unsurprised when after a great deal of splashing and barking my black lab, Ted, emerged from the weeds at the side of the creek with a large, dark king salmon in his jaws. I'd like to have witnessed the catch. The end result was no less spectacular than a brown bear snatching a salmon from the Kenai River. Salmon, despite their popularity in these parts, aren't all that hard to catch. Ask Ted.

As a more serious fishing adult, I developed a few techniques that increased my skinny-water salmonid hookup rates both for salmon and rainbows. To begin with, I employ the blue-heron method of observing before pursuing. Standing back from the creek, I watch to see where the heaviest fish activity is. Freshly into the creek, the steelhead often shoot up and down in twenty or thirty yard sprints, the males chasing each other off in preparation for the coming weeks' spawning. I try not to mess with the spawning females and I don't fish them once the spawn is under way. Much as I do with gar fishing, I like to find a single fish (usually a male) that's located some distance away from the others. As with sight fishing for gar, I find having only *one* set of eyes as you make the approach decreases the likelihood of scaring a pod of fish off *en masse*.

Quietly watching the activity, I estimated that a half-dozen fish were already in the pool. After a few more moments of blue-heron-like stalking, I locked onto a small pool behind a downed branch. Every now and then the silvery back of the male steelhead showed as he finned in impossibly shallow water. I knelt in the mud and crawled thirty or forty yards down the creek. At one point, a large female erupted from a short gravely run. All of ten pounds, how she remained concealed in ten inches of clear water is beyond my comprehension. A giant silver fish shouldn't be a model of natural camouflage. Thankfully, she raced in the opposite direction of my stalk. Approaching my target, I clearly saw his back sticking out of the water, now just a bit further down the creek and squeezing into even shallower water.

Part of my technique is to not over-cast. There's not much room for error in this very small creek and one cast too many can result in instant failure as the fish—with nowhere else to go—race off down the creek, often for hundreds of yards.

Pulling the fly free from the wire loop, I quickly zipped off twenty feet of line. Still on my knees, I false cast once over the trout, adjusted and dropped the white Woolly Bugger three feet upstream. There was a quick flash as the trout adjusted an inch or two to intercept the fly. He was on! I raised the rod tip and the small male steelhead flipped out of the water. While the giant females are bruising battlers on the line, the little males are much more entertaining with their aerial acrobatics and speed. This one did not disappoint, leaping out of the water three times and vibrating like a live wire. It was all I could do to hang on. After taking a brief break behind the same log from which he'd come, the trout pursued a different tactic. I thought he was starting to tire and applied a bit more pressure. That was all it took and he was off to the submarine races. One side of the creek is choked with trees and the other is relatively open. As so very often happens in this miniature stretch of water, the trout headed north as fast as he could. My only option was running through the creek, jumping onto the bank on the clear side, and running after him. Of the very few fish I've ever broken off here, this is how they'd always managed to do it. I may have been rusty after a year, but I quickly recalled past lessons. This time, I managed to *run* in my chest waders, slip-sliding through the March mud as line peeled off my reel in a mechanical buzz. Easily racing to the next deep pool with me in tow like an earthbound kite, the trout stopped only briefly. The pool suddenly erupted as a dozen fish scattered in all directions. Some went south, back toward my house and others went north. Among them was *my* fish, though in the melee I had no idea which was mine. I kept running. At one point my line grew slack and I assumed I'd lost him. Planting my feet in the mud, I reeled as fast as my shaking hands would allow. The reel again doled out line, clacking maddeningly. *He's still on!* I ran again, this time with less enthusiasm. Out of shape from my winter of sluggishness, I began contemplating not if but *when* this fish was going to run me either out of line or out of energy. We'd covered better than a hundred yards already and he showed no signs of slowing. Farther downstream, the creek took a hard left and, thankfully, that seemed to be the trout's selection for his final stand. With a few headshakes and one last leap, he finally tired. Since he didn't seem to want to go any further north than the bend, I unhooked my net and stepped into the creek. Not knowing how much damage my leader had sustained, I didn't want to force the fish, but at some point you always have to. I applied firm pressure to the rod and dropped my net into the water, across the current. As I suspected, the feisty male steelhead took one last run—this time straight at me. It's a favorite tactic of these big trout when confined in small water and one that has lost me plenty of fish. As he neared, and prepared to shoot past me on the left, I interrupted by placing the big rubber net in his path.

Obligingly (which isn't always the case), he swam into it.

A small male steelhead would be considered a *big trout* in most waters. Whether they're native or not, they are beautiful creatures. Still dressed in the polished chrome of a fresh run fish, in a week or two he'd exhibit a deep red streak, more like a true small-stream rainbow. Either color phase is a natural work of art, though I prefer the chrome. A *chromer* (as the locals call them) represents the onset of the new season, one full of hope and power and things that might be. As much as the new red twigs and green buds hint at the imminent onset of spring, so does that bright silver. I watched the fish swim off. He didn't go far before selecting another log behind which he could hide. He had certainly earned the rest.

I didn't bother fishing anymore. We'd so disrupted two of the main fishable pools I figured resting them until tomorrow might be the wisest plan. No rush. The run was just getting started. If I were a younger man, I would have fished the hell out of the little creek until the last tendril of daylight disappeared from the western sky and my arms were tired from casting. Not anymore. I walked home slowly (no trotting this time), content in the knowledge that the fish would be there again tomorrow.

Silver Lake

I've always liked northern pike. My first big fish was a northern pike caught on a bobber and worm at Loon Lake, in the Adirondack Mountains. I was ten years old. If Twelve-Mile Creek was the headwaters of my life (and my fishing life), Loon Lake was the source water for my enthusiastic pursuit of toothy predator fish. It's simply a love affair that never ended, both with Loon Lake and with northern pike.

While my home water is home to some great pike fishing, this past summer Lake Ontario levels were higher than they'd been since 1952. Flooding, damage and shore erosion were unlike anything seen in a generation. It wasn't just the lake. The tributaries suffered as well. Docks were submerged under two feet (and often more) of water, making water hazards and rendering old, familiar waters into alien landscapes. *My creek had spread out past its banks and up into the woods in many places.* Boat launches were completely submerged, as well as their parking lots in some places. That, coupled with the murky conditions augmented by the flooding, made for dangerous boating and less than ideal fishing. The pike bug, as it does almost every year, had bitten me and I wasn't going to be happy until I pulled a big, smiling pike or two onto the deck of my small kayak. I waited longer than I normally do for the pike fishing, hoping for the lake levels to recede a bit. When they went the opposite way, I formulated Plan B.

The six-month anniversary of Jen's death came and went with May 2nd. Every 2nd day of every month was hard, but the six-month mark seemed to usher in a colder, darker reality of life without my youngest daughter. We all felt it. My fishing distraction had been the only thing keeping my sanity. Now, with the flooded lake levels, I felt that sanity slipping away.

Time to enact Fishing Plan B.

With such a wonderful fishery only four miles from my home (and occasionally running through my back yard), it always seems silly to travel *too* far to chase fish that I could easily be catching closer to home. That said, Lake Ontario wasn't nearing fishability fast enough for me. After a quick bit of research and contacting a few other predator aficionados, I settled on Silver Lake. Located an hour's drive south of my home, it's a small lake known for its big pike and bass. I hadn't fished it in years. I couldn't even tell you how many years. Fifteen? *Twenty?* But it is the place that two of my three friends suggested as a good kayak-fishing destination: small enough to be small-boat friendly, but big enough to hold large pike. Good enough for me.

The drive down through Western New York's farm country was a pleasant one. I found myself less lost in my own thoughts and more in the moment as the flat land of my hometown gave way to the rolling hills of Wyoming County. I vaguely recalled launching at the state launch last time I was here, but wouldn't wager any large sums of money on the accuracy of that memory. At one of my friends' suggestions, I launched at a small marina at the north end of the lake. The old couple that ran the marina (which was just their house and a small concrete ramp) were more than happy to come out and make conversation. That alone was worth the $5 launch fee. They did, however, seem disappointed that I was there to target pike.

"Really? You're not here for calicos?"

Silver Lake is renowned in some circles for its pike and bass, but apparently more so for its black crappie fishing. Black crappie or *calicos,* as the locals call them, grow large and plentiful in Silver Lake, and are probably targeted more than bass and pike combined.

"Yep, just going for pike."

They seemed disappointed. *Story of my life.*

The small group of homes quickly vanished behind me as I paddled out the narrow channel toward the lake. The tree canopy closed overhead and I briefly had the sensation of being in a remote wilderness, with only the emerging wood ferns and underbrush lining the banks. It was one of the more serene paddling experiences I'd had so far in this young fishing season. Passing over a deep pool, I paused and cast a large, deep-diving crankbait, hoping to entice any pike that may still be spawning in the creek. I wasn't surprised when, on the second or third cast, a very respectable largemouth bass slammed the big lure. After handling and releasing the bass, my fingers were extremely cold. Even down in the hill country, a thirty-nine degree morning in May is unseasonably cold. In my case, it was also a bit unexpected and I suddenly wished I'd dressed warmer. I cast a while longer in the deep pool, pulling out a smaller bass that had no business hitting a lure almost as large as he was.

When the inlet (or is it the *outlet*…I can't remember) spread out onto the open lake, the illusion of remoteness vaporized. Cabins and summer homes dotted the shoreline, though the north end remained fairly uncivilized. Submerged branches and willows lined the northeast corner. I chose to stay there for a while. It felt fishy.

After blowing some hot breath into my cold hands, I laid my two primary pike fishing rods out on the deck of the kayak: a bait-caster with a spinnerbait on the left and a baitcaster with the large crankbait on the right. I've done well with this pairing. Pike are often aggressive enough to hit twice, but I've found they're *more* likely to hit twice *if* the presentation is altered—quickly—between the first miss and the next strike. This one-two punch has landed me many pike that might otherwise have disappeared after the first strike and miss.

There was no difficulty in selecting the first rod. I picked the spinnerbait. A heavy spinnerbait with a muskie-tail added to it has been potent medicine for northern pike wherever I've fished for them. That lure has also resulted in some of the biggest bass of my career. It's my go-to lure in most shallow water situations, and always instills confidence beyond my abilities. Magic, in other words. I couldn't find any reason to start with anything else. I usually can't.

With a gentle south wind rocking the kayak, I cast toward the willow roots to the north. Overshooting my mark (let's blame it on cold fingers), the spinnerbait landed in the crotch of one of the stunted willows. Feeling that it was hopelessly tangled and assuming that I'd simply have to paddle ashore to retrieve it, I nonetheless gave a hopeful yank and the white spinnerbait popped free and plopped into the water several yards from the roots. Almost as soon as I began reeling, a savage strike nearly ripped the rod from my unprepared hands. The pike cartwheeled as I tried to regain my composure. Several times, the northern came out of the water. There really was no other option, I'd hooked him in less than a foot of water. Where else would he go? As far as game fish go, pike's savagery usually uses itself up rather quickly and they are not *that hard* to bring in. Most pike lost are a result of those razor teeth cutting through insufficient test line, not due to their endurance. I love pike, but they tend to give up rather easily. Most of them, anyway. After battling steelhead and salmon on small streams, pike don't scare me. They're one of my favorite fish, so I don't begrudge them a little laziness.

This pike was fat, but not huge. I was pleased as could be with my first northern of the year. I didn't bother with the net, rather lifting him by the spinnerbait into the kayak. Once on deck, I realized I'd underestimated him. Not quite three-feet, he was still a very nice fish. I quickly switched on the GoPro for a photo and released him. Drying off my rapidly numbing hands, I began casting again. No more than a dozen casts later, a hammer-handle pike came to the boat. Much smaller but even more acrobatic than the first pike, I didn't bother with pictures, just pleased to have my second fish in the boat in just a matter of minutes.

If the morning had ended there, I would have been satisfied. Three or four more fish, none more than two feet, also found the spinnerbait irresistible. It was a very good first hour of fishing. I later told people I caught six fish in that first location, but I don't really know. It could have been seven. Might have been five. Six is a good number.

When the south wind picked up well into the second hour of fishing, I found myself struggling with the kayak, constantly drifting into the roots and weeds from which I'd been pulling the pike. It became a chore. *Cast, paddle, cast, paddle.* Even though I hoped to pull a few more fish out of this very productive spot, I'd had enough of a workout. Seeking both to explore this newly rediscovered lake as well as get the kayak in out of the wind, I made a short paddle to a sheltered cove. With the summer season not yet under way, the sandy shallows were just beginning to show emergent vegetation and it looked pretty pikelike to me.

I still hadn't touched the second rod and considered briefly casting the crankbait instead of the spinnerbait. *Why,* asked the little voice inside my head. *Why indeed,* said the bigger voice. I cast the spinnerbait out toward nothing in particular. A streak behind it against the sandy backdrop appeared to be a big fish. Another streak came from my left. *Two!* As the fish neared the boat, I slowed the crankbait, hoping to entice one of them into a strike. Anyone who's ever had a pike (or two) savagely rush the boat only to pause without striking knows the frustration. In a brief flash of inspiration, I considered doing a figure-8 maneuver with the lure. Before I could execute it, though, both fish vanished. I saw which way the larger of the two went and quickly grabbed my second rod, still dry from disuse. I lobbed the heavy lure in what I presumed was the general vicinity the pike was headed. It was met with a smashing hit almost as soon as it hit the water. The pike did not tail-walk nor take to the air at all. *Bingo.* This was a big fish.

Still only in two feet of water, I couldn't make out the pike quite yet but could clearly feel its large headshakes. He wasn't covering ground. He was just duking it out. If his smaller cousins were lazy, he was not.

I minded the line pressure, hoping not to let him saw through the monofilament with each turn of his head. Inch by inch, I slowly pulled him my way. When the pike reached the side of the boat, I could now see what I already knew—he was a big fish. Probably forty-plus inches, he grinned that malevolent grin as I lowered my big net in front of him. In a sizzle of drag, the pike ran twenty yards of line out, surprising me. I inched him back in. At the side of the boat, this time he seemed tired but I watched him warily, waiting for another explosive run. I have several fishing rules. I don't regularly abide by many of them, though I should. They are *good* rules. One of them involves my nasty photography habit. To me a nice fish *must* be photographed. I've always been a photographer and always insisted on fish pictures to document good catches for the purpose of being able to relive them months or years later. With the technology currently available, including wireless remotes and phone-apps, there's no reason not to get a good photo of a great fish. My kayak is generally outfitted with one or two GoPro cameras within easy reach. I have them set, at various times, to either record time-lapse photos or video. Often both. Getting back to the *rules,* my rule about photography is simple: Don't mess with the camera until the fish is in the boat. I've lost more fish when turning on a camera than for almost any other reason. With bass and panfish, it doesn't matter all that much. However, with the bigger, feistier fish, taking your attention off them at the last minute is a recipe for disaster.

In clear violation of the rules and with the big pike still parallel to the kayak, I switched my rod from left to right hand, and switched on the GoPro, which began snapping away as evidenced by the blinking red LED. The pike took that opportunity to make an unlikely *second* run while my fishing rod languished in my wrong hand—my *stupid* hand. As line peeled out, I panicked, switching the rod back to my smart hand and cursing my own stupidity. It wasn't just my hand! I managed to haul the pike back to the kayak yet again. He still had a surprising amount of fight left and eyed me murderously upon our latest (and final) meeting.

Switching hands yet again, I grabbed the big landing net and slipped it under and around the big pike. He more than filled the net. Overthinking or perhaps *underthinking* things, I reached into the net and dislodged the big spinnerbait, keeping my fingers as clear of those teeth as I possibly could and still get the job done. Once he was free of the hook, I lifted the net from the water to hold him up for at least one photo. When the pike felt the pressure of the net against his belly, though, he made two mighty flops in the net. His weight was not inconsiderable. Suddenly, the kayak rocked as I struggled to heave the net over the gunnels with one hand. It didn't work. Another muscular flip and flop and suddenly the pike was airborne, above the net and then gone. When I reviewed the photos that night at home, they were pretty comical. Nowhere in them was anything that resembled a northern pike. Mostly there was just epic splashing followed by me holding an empty net with a less-than-pleased look on my face. *What a brawl!*

I've always liked northern pike.

Invasive Species

I didn't know what was on the line. The golden fish flashing and catching the light just below the murky surface of my creek could have been just about anything. One moment, it seemed to be a large, mutant shiner. Another glimpse revealed some red coloration that suggested a common goldfish. It was big, as panfish go. At least twelve inches in length, the flashy fish put up a good fight. Bending the ultra-light spinning rod over double, I swung the fish into the kayak. Upon closer inspection, it *seemed* to be a golden shiner and was certainly minnow-like in most of its physical attributes. But the body color was wrong. Its golden hue was quite bright —almost a pale gold—and its fins had brilliant red highlights. It was the first time in a long time that I had no idea what I'd caught on my home water. Switching on the GoPro, I held up the fish for a moment or two as the camera snapped away. Turning it this way and that, to secure a good photo-record of the mystery catch, I didn't ponder too briefly before returning it to the water. In the same small area between two downed trees, I caught three more of the colorful fighters, though none was as big as the first. Later at home, I looked up the mystery fish. Eurasian rudd. The first article I found online referred to it distastefully as an *invasive species*. Depending on the source material I read, it either was introduced into North American waters as a gamefish, a food-fish, or a baitfish. I didn't much care how it got here. I was just glad to know what it was.

Another article went on to say that some fishery biologists feel that the rudd is cross-breeding with the native golden shiners, to whom they bear a great resemblance.

Whatever the true story (or stories) of the rudd's introduction, it's not so dissimilar from the introduction of hundreds of other species over the last few hundred years. Almost all, with few exceptions, are the result of human introduction. The Great Lakes, including *my* Great Lake, are the breeding grounds for a great many species that weren't here a thousand years ago. Bait gone wild along with hitchhikers in the ballast water of countless ocean-going vessels all contributed to our current ecosystem. Then there's the purposeful stocking by sport fishermen of their favorite species from one area to another. Also, released aquarium fish along with a host of other methods have made the bio-diversity in our waterways even more interesting than nature intended.

I have mixed feelings on *invasive species*. Oh, I know there are invaders that have done harm to our sometimes-fragile ecosystem, such as zebra mussels and various kinds of aquatic vegetation. Their damage is real and measurable. I don't think invasive species' destructiveness is the rule, so much as the exception. I'm not a fan of the broad-brush approach when it comes to anything ecological, and that's just as true regarding invasive species.

When I read various states' literature and reports on invasive species, it's often hard to ignore the hypocrisy. While nature may not have intended for Eurasian rudd, round goby, European carp, goldfish and others to make the Great Lakes watersheds their home, they have. Are those fish any more or less acceptable than the giant king salmon cruising the depths and creeks that are the source of so much of our local fishing economy? What about the alewives that were introduced, thereby knocking off the balance of the *natural* forage fish? They've been in the Great Lakes since the 1800's. When do they stop being invasive and start being accepted as a part of the modern aquascape? Where do we draw the line? Brown trout? No one even thinks about brown trout being of

European origins. They are such a part of Americana and American fishing lore that few know and even fewer fishermen likely care that they are, by definition, an invasive species. I wouldn't like to give up the thrill of catching a fall-run brown trout on a small fly. Besides, there's no way to go back. They may have *been* invasive, but now they're here to stay.

While we're talking brown trout, let's talk about the round goby. The goby is a tiny, aggressive and somewhat comical fish. If I were going to create (if I could draw—and I can't—one of the reasons I'm a photographer*!*) a cartoon fish it would be the goby. How did the round goby get into Lake Ontario and my home creeks? Well, a funny thing happened. Some agencies thought it would be good to *introduce* them to help control the burgeoning zebra mussel population. That's right, they introduced an aggressive non-native species to help control a prolific non-native species. This, unfortunately, worked out like it usually does: Poorly. Oh, they'll eat zebra mussels but, no surprise, they also disrupted the native mussel population by dining on them as well. Did no one consider that might happen? Now, on a calm day, I can walk out on one of the Lake Ontario piers near my home and peer down into eight or ten feet of water and see the new alien landscape. There are round gobies and zebra mussels everywhere. Every now and then a carp swims by too.

Enter the brown trout. On Lake Ontario, we have some of the biggest brown trout (non-native) in the world. Though not as exciting as the king salmon (non-native) that are far more often the target of pursuit, they are increasingly targeted. Trollers and deep-water fishermen can get them most of the year, but they're also prized during the fall runs. Guess what the big brown trout like to eat. Can you? Yes, *round gobies*. It makes the head spin. The browns seem to have quickly adapted to eating the gobies. I don't keep or eat the fish out of the lake anymore, but several charter captain friends have told me it's not uncommon to find the stomachs of brown trout and salmonids stuffed full of round gobies. Win-win? I don't know. You decide.

A lot has been written on the destructiveness of the carp, introduced here as a game fish and (less successfully) as a food fish. I've read for years about them eating game fish eggs and being generally bad for the environment. However, as long as I've been fishing Twelve-Mile Creek, I've seen the ponderous, massive carp alongside bass and pike that don't seem to mind sharing the water. The twenty and sometimes thirty-pound carp have finally, after many years, started to attract a small but loyal fan base here in the tributaries. What is not to like about a fish of that size that can be consistently taken on light tackle? And to eradicate them is out of the question, so I don't understand the labeling of *trash fish* and *garbage fish* that I so often hear. How can a fifteen-pound catfish be a trophy while a fifteen-pound carp is saddled with the unfortunate designation as *trash fish?* I'll be the first to tell you I have a great deal of affection for the rough fish (the nice name for trash fish), so my perception may perhaps be skewed, but I still don't get it.

Invasive species.

While we're talking carp, how about the silver carp? Known colloquially as the *flying carp*, they're one of the rising stars of the invasive species movement. Their defense mechanism, when startled, is to leap high above the water, often in large groups. Funny thing is (you've probably seen the videos), they are frequently startled *by boats.* Leaping to the air in great numbers, they commonly end up flying into boats (fishing and pleasure boats alike!), very often whacking people in the head. Now, the silver carp is not the same as a tiny round goby. They can reach three-feet in length. *Whack!* As an invasive species, they're not very good at staying quiet about their invasion. A recent study in a small part of the Ohio River watershed put their population density at incalculable numbers. They invaded, and they appear to have won. How did the flying carp get here? They were introduced into aquaculture and municipal wastewater facilities in the 1970s to help control algae growth. *Oops.* The population, despite many efforts at prevention by fish and wildlife agencies, has steadily moved north. They're disruptive to native fish populations but, at this point, there doesn't seem to be much we can do now but complain about it. There's an idea being floated now to introduce alligator gar into several watersheds to possibly help mitigate the silver carp population. What could possibly go wrong!?

Round and round we go.

I could cite for you any number of invasive species. They're all around. As I stated earlier, my local waterways don't seem to be too upset by their presence. The bass and pike and panfish still make their livings, providing me with hours of entertainment. Even the gar and bowfin, survivors of millions of years of invasion and attrition, are doing okay *thank you very much.* I suppose it doesn't seem like I'm taking invasive species very seriously. I do, but also feel the cat is out of the bag and, using the example of the brown trout adapting to feeding on the round goby, nature always seems to find a way to reach a new balance. Undoubtedly, some natural fish populations in critical watersheds have suffered from the introduction of invaders. In a big, robust fishery like Lake Ontario, however, there's always a little more room for someone new and there's usually somebody out there willing to eat them.

A friend recently said that Lake Ontario is no longer a natural fishery. I'm not quick to agree with that statement. What is natural? If a bird flies in from South America with fish eggs attached to its feet (a very common vector for fish eggs), if those fish suddenly hatch in southern Florida and move steadily northward over the next hundred years, is that an invasive species? Or is it simply one spread by nature doing its thing and filling every niche? If it displaces a native fish, is that not a natural occurrence? Then, the question becomes, if a species is manipulated and introduced (accidentally or with good intentions) by *humans,* is it any less natural? Are we not part of the natural world? The same people who would say yes may argue contrarily that we are *not.* I feel that we are. I realize a species spreading slowly and steadily in one direction or the other, adapting as it overtakes new territory is *not* the same as a hitchhiker in the bow of a ship from China entering the Great Lakes. There's bound to be trouble, but it seems that every effort at mitigation gets us into more trouble. I, for one, am looking forward to a future full of giant alligator gar, well fed on flying carp, making their way to my home water. I'm already working on the lures—and maybe a bigger kayak.

Invasive species. What's the answer? I don't know. Goby tournaments with tiny scales for the weigh-in? Silver carp fish-fries? Perhaps. To get the answer, though, we have to ask some different, more existential questions. Most importantly among them: What is *natural?*

Oh, if you're waiting for me to answer that, remember one thing. I'm just a fisherman!

Strong is the Current

Twelve-Mile Creek is nothing special. Meandering from a hundred drainage ditches in a dozen farmers' fields far above before forming finally into a single definitive flow, it is not heralded in any angling circles. Though it has all of the species found in the more popular area creeks—salmon, steelhead, bass, pike etc.—their runs are brief and unspectacular and very often uncooperative. It's a muddy, murky, mundane and often distasteful tributary. Nobody is jockeying one's boat for fishing position in my creek. Is it a diamond in the rough? No. Not really. It's just rough. Shallow, weedy, poorly oxygenated and very seldom spectacular, it's the kind of place I feel comfortable calling my own. Once late July and August are upon us, there's not always enough water to fish anywhere but the lower reaches near the mouth of Lake Ontario. Very often, those lower stretches become so choked with vegetation and duckweed that maneuvering even my small kayak turns into an exercise in futility.

These days, though, Twelve-Mile Creek has become something of a voyage into the past for me. A "tributary time machine," if you will—and maybe you won't. For me, it always has been a voyage in time, but now these fishing trips to the past are more poignant, far less abstract. Much like the many species that muck out their existence in the creek and on its mostly inaccessible banks, I need it to survive. That's truer now than ever.

If I really wanted to be serious and detailed about this tributary time machine, I'd tell you that I was born on the banks of this unimpressive creek. Ransomville General Hospital is a figment of the past. Once a booming local hospital, it's now a retirement home. The last name I was aware of was Heritage Manor, though I'm sure it's something different by now. I haven't checked the sign lately. I was born a few yards away from the drainage ditch that served as the outlet for the septic tank for Ransomville General Hospital. That ditch fed another drainage ditch, and then another, and then Twelve-Mile Creek.

When I was a very young kid—in second grade—the creek was a source of fun, frolic and fantasy. Around 1975, my best friend David (whose grandfather had been a legendary doctor at Ransomville General Hospital) and I spent many of our days catching frogs, spearing suckers and pretending that we were the *Six-Million Dollar Man*. What a wonderful time to be alive. No cell phones. No computer games. All we had was a cheesy television show with bad actors to keep our imaginations ignited and our daydreams fulfilled. It worked. *It worked*!

Mere yards from where David and I acted out our sci-fi visions of a future ushered in by Steve Austin, forty years later I've taken up the latest chapter of my life. I can't tell you how many steelhead and salmon I've caught on the banks of the very small creek that used to serve as the soundstage to two very fertile young minds. Traversing farther down the creek, my third-grade friend (who would later become my best friend long after David had moved away) would set out to float from our small hometown of Ransomville to the bigger water far below in Wilson. Frank was my best friend from third grade all the way through high school. Our adventures ranged from canoeing and fishing Twelve-Mile Creek, all the way to the Catskill Mountains when one fateful train ride to visit Frank's grandfather would point me in the direction of fishing and the outdoors for life. For now, though, high up on the creek, our young adventures involved hiking and exploring.

Later on, Frank and I would take his father's canoe far down the tributary, all the way from our hometown to Lake Ontario. On one misadventure, we capsized the canoe in icy water somewhere between Ransomville and Wilson, and it's not much of an exaggeration to say we could have died. We were at the time, however, much more concerned with saving Frank's dad's canoe. We didn't perish, nor were we beaten to death. In high school Frank and I took to fishing the other side of Twelve-Mile Creek, the West Branch. We did pretty well catching bass and pike, but one day an explosive eel-like creature slammed my chartreuse spinnerbait. The three-foot fish crashed and banged and flipped around the inside of the canoe until it finally freed itself of the spinnerbait's single hook and flipped out over the side, with a helping left hand from Frank, if I recall correctly.

"What the hell was that?" Both of us yelled.

Thus began my love affair with not only the bowfin (*Amia Calva* is the Latin name, and it goes by so many other regional names that I figured I better give you the Latin so you know what I'm talking about), but also with all of the rough fish. Our area, so renowned for the salmon and steelhead, huge smallmouth bass, pike, walleye and muskie, is also blessed with *big* dino-fish. Longnose gar pushing four feet are common in several waterways and have lately become my personal favorite. Carp upwards of thirty pounds are not at all uncommon. Sheepshead (freshwater drum) are the bane of many bass fishermen, but also tip the scale in excess of twenty pounds from time to time, and fight like devils too. Like most Great Lakes tributaries, mine has a dizzying array of species—if you can get to them—and at one time or another, I've fished for them all.

Farther down the river of time, you would very likely find me wading with my fly rod for bass and panfish under the Lake Road bridge, listening to the coos and echoes of the bridge pigeons and the occasional rumble of car and truck traffic on the steel deck above. Even on the hottest days, in the shade of the bridge and up to my waist in the questionable water, I found cool relief after a day of school or picking tomatoes on a local farm. I wasn't afraid to bike the short distance between my childhood home and the bridge, but once I had my driver's license I was there all the time.

As this time flow continued, you'd find my young family. Jessica and Jennifer fished the tiny public fishing docks, catching their first fish from the murky depths of my home water at a very young age. They were four and seven when I hooked a respectable bowfin. Fishing worms and bobbers, I'll never forget their faces when I hauled the bowfin up onto the old concrete boat launch. Glowing iridescent green in its spring breeding colors, the fish wasn't very big, but it was imposing with those toxic-avenger colors, the eyespot on its tail and its dog like face. As expected, Jessica took several steps backward away from the slimy, squirming dinosaur and Jennifer took several steps forward, nearly getting whacked in the forehead while I tried to unhook it. That was the place that sealed Jen's love of fishing (and it could very well be that bowfin that sealed Jessica's *dislike* of fishing, come to think of it!). The creek would come into play later in my kids' lives, as well. Traumatized by my divorce from their mom, Jennifer took it the hardest. The year she barely spoke to me can never be earned back and can never be made up. I lost a year in estrangement that we didn't have to lose.

Twelve-Mile Creek, though, had a place in the healing of that rift. After a particularly tense few months of getting no responses to my calls, texts and emails (it isn't easy being the child of a writer), my phone rang one day out of the blue, and it was Jen. She'd bought a new kayak and wanted to go out with me. We both enjoyed kayaking and we both loved fishing. Twelve-Mile Creek just happened to be exactly halfway between her house and mine. It's also where we met halfway. The first day—a warm day in early May when the pike were hitting very well—there wasn't a lot of talk. It was good to be Dad again, helping her to unhook her fish and talking about the birds and photography and her plans for the future. I can still hear her voice, excited with the prospects of new jobs and new ventures. She wanted to start a dog-rescue operation.

We talked for hours about a future that would never be.

As the summer passed, we kayak fished several different places together, but most often on Twelve-Mile Creek. Each trip, the conversation flowed more easily as she accepted me back in to her life. Jennifer was a person who felt things very deeply, very passionately, and was not afraid to say what was on her mind, though it often took some coaxing. When she had finally forgiven me, realizing I was the same person I'd always been and I'd always be there for her, she let me know it. If she hadn't, I don't know where I'd be right now. That Father's Day, we all kayaked in the creek. It was a perfect day. In the years following our reconciliation, Jennifer would come to rely more and more on all of us as her condition deteriorated. Jen and I were okay long before that. There's something about the backdrop of nature, the silence and the water. *Always the water.*

Several bass came to the kayak as I floated my old home water, pondering my personal history on that creek. It always seems the less mentally engaged in the fishing I am, the better the bite. Sitting at the mouth just a few yards from Lake Ontario, I turned the kayak back toward the bridge, but I didn't paddle. I put the rods back in their holders behind me. I stood in the kayak, stretching my legs and back after a long afternoon fishing. Facing upstream, I tried to picture each event from the upper reaches of my youth to the passing of the torch to my daughter. I can think of a hundred more stories, stretched out over the better part of five decades from the time I was a young boy catching my first fish here to my kids catching their first fish. My mind drifted as well to friends and family, laughter and memories.

If I could paddle on through time, what would I find? Probably the same old creek, going about its same old business as it passes through fields and woods, finally emptying into Lake Ontario, wholly unconcerned with such nonsensically human issues as *time*. It's fitting that the upper reaches of the past were choked now with weeds and the open expanse of lake is a bit too rough to explore the future. For now, I was forced to stay in the now. My todays hadn't been too great lately; but here, at least, they were tolerable.

A green heron landed a few yards from me. Perching on a low branch, he began his afternoon fishing. Reaching behind me for a fishing rod, I proceeded to do the same. It was time to get out of my head for a while, as much as that was possible. The heavy minnow lure arced out over the water, splashing down next to a mostly submerged stump. Glancing at the heron before I began the retrieve, I noted his patience and tried to emulate it.

I'm still trying.

Fishing Notes—April 29th, 2003

Bad case of hives. Should <u>never</u> have cleaned the gutters. Fished Oatka Creek, loopy on Benadryl. Clear & warm with a cool north breeze. Cars at every parking space on the trail. No doubt that the hatches have begun. Still, it was a pretty thick crowd for a Tuesday morning.

Highlights:

- *Caught a 16 inch brown on a 16 Hendrikson. Beautiful fish! Fat & colorful.*

- *Landed 8 trout. 2 others were decent, but short of the 16". All on dry flies. Not bad for early afternoon!.*

- *A guy about my age asked me what the size limit was on trout. I told him 16 inches. Total lie. It's 12. He believed me! Haha. Didn't see him again.*

- *Started itching again. By the time I got home I was covered in hives again. Looked like a zombie, but at least I was a zombie who landed 8 trout!*

First Loves, First Fish

Five or six years before Jennifer's illness, I hadn't fly-fished for steelhead in a very long time. For many years, it had been an obsession of mine, but one from which I'd gotten away. I don't know if it was distraction with other interests, boredom, or the fact that one of my favorite fishing places had become so well known that it was impossible to have a peaceful morning on the stream. Regardless, I'd given it up except for a few sporadic trips.

The steelhead runs in the Lake Ontario tributaries, including my home water, can be spectacular. The larger the stream, the more fabulous they tend to be. As a kid (and to this day) I was more interested in the natural fishes, like northern pike, bowfin and others, but there's an undeniable rush in hooking a big steelhead, salmon or brown trout on the fly rod on a small stream no matter how artificial their introduction. By *big*, I mean thirty-inches, and often more. It took me decades to learn how to consistently land a twelve-pound fish on four-pound test line, but I've gotten pretty adept at it. It's more art than science and technique. No matter that the fish had been stocked years ago and their runs would probably perish from this earth without the aid and comfort of the New York State Department of Environmental Conservation, they are still an awful lot of fun. And, despite their hatchery lineage, they're every bit as big and beautiful as their wild western counterparts. If you've never hooked a steelhead rainbow trout in skinny water, put it on your list.

To get back into it, I requested a new fly rod and reel for my birthday the summer before. Nice fly rod setups aren't cheap, and getting one as a gift would almost guarantee that I'd feel obliged to use it. That feeling of obligation didn't last long and it only took one trip to rekindle my former love of small stream steelheading.

The first outing didn't go well. I spotted two of the big silver fish finning in six inch deep water, barely enough to keep them covered. My first clumsy cast sent them upstream. I followed, but never found them. I wore out my elbow casting to the deeper pools, rewarded only with a big brown sucker. Still, being the naturalist that I am, the sucker was a pretty good trophy and I wasn't above posing for a quick self-timer photo before releasing the rubber-lipped rough fish. Though it was March and the days were getting progressively longer, sunset approached rapidly and the stream appeared devoid of all but those two big trout. I casually cast my way back toward the road, thinking I might for once get home in time for dinner. Lost in thought, I only noticed I had a fish on when the *snick* of the line through my guides grabbed my attention. Lifting the rod tip as if I hadn't been years out of practice, I hooked a small male. Small male steelhead rainbow trout are much more fun than their big sisters and uncles. While the big fish tend to stay submerged and run like a high-speed freight train, it's the smaller ones that put on the best show. Taking to the air almost immediately, the seventeen-inch fish leapt from the water. Before descending, he reached eye level with me and his chrome color and red sides shone above the little creek. *Unlike* the big fish, he came pretty easily to the net, horsed in without too much effort. I unhooked him underwater and watched as he swam free. I realized that was my first steelhead in a good number of years. I also realized why I used to be obsessed with steelhead fishing. It's good, explosive fun.

The early spring sun dipped low in the west cutting an orange disk through the distant wood lot. I decided to make for the road before darkness enveloped me. Cutting through the woods, I heard the unmistakable sound of youthful laughter and frantic splashing in the creek to my west, and couldn't resist investigating. I arrived just as a young couple netted a large female steelhead.

Walking up behind them, I whistled to let them know I was there.

As I get older, I find it harder to judge ages, but I think they were probably seventeen. The girl was the catcher, and the boy was the netter. As much as I enjoy encountering strangers out in the wilds, you never know how they'll respond to someone else showing up. Hell, I never know how *I* will respond.

"Hey!" The boy shouted when he saw me.

"Awesome fish!" I shouted back. I'm sure that "awesome" isn't a thing anymore and that I sounded like I'd just walked out of a 1980s movie.

"Check this out," he said. "She said 'steelhead fishing is *easy!*'"

"It is!" The girl said, laughing.

We were all laughing.

"Would you take our photo?"

"Of course," I said as he handed me his phone. I felt like an antique, having an actual *camera* in my fishing pack.

Until then, they'd held the big trout underwater in the net. The boy, playing the gentleman as much as possible, scooped it out of the net, unhooked it and proceeded to hand it to the girl. Being a steelhead—the prizefighter of all fish—the big hen didn't respond well. Twisting and turning, she fought hard to make them drop her, an arm wrestling match between two diverse species. The girl got the fish firmly in her grasp, if only briefly, and I snapped (can you really *snap* anymore?) a couple of photos on the boy's phone. Without a word, the boy took the fish and lowered it into the water to revive it. It only took a second. With a splash, the steelhead was gone in a flash of silver.

The girl, who hadn't said much, said, "That was my first fish!"

Awesome, I thought. "Congratulations," I said.

"And she says steelhead fishing is easy!" The boy repeated.

"Isn't it, though?"

It took a minute, but he finally realized I was joking and once again we all laughed. What a great thing to be seventeen with your whole life ahead of you and helping your girl land her first trout.

I wished them a good afternoon, but inside I wished them a good life.

Checking off the Boxes

The longnose gar (*Lepistosteus osseus*) is an interesting creature. Though its larger cousin the alligator gar has earned some sport fishing respect lately, the longnose gar—the only gar in New York— remains an obscure fish and one that very few locals (and from what I've read, almost *anyone)* pursue. I'm okay with that. The longnose gar is a long, thin fish. While the alligator gar can reach six or even seven feet, the longnose can still reach an impressive five feet in length and I've caught several in the neighborhood of four feet. While a four-foot gar may weigh twelve pounds, its thin profile keeps it from the impressive weights reached by pike and muskie that share the gar's home range. A four-foot pike runs about twice the weight of a four-foot gar. Still, a four-foot toothy fish (especially in a ten or twelve foot kayak) is an interesting prospect—to me anyway. The gar's most distinct visual characteristics are its heavy scales that serve to act as interlocking armor plating and, more impressive, its long beak.

Gar have the ability, like the bowfin, to breathe air. Their modified swim bladder can be used as a primitive lung, allowing them to gulp air at the surface. This ability to breathe in poorly oxygenated water has undoubtedly led to both species' evolutionary longevity. It's an amazing sight to see those long beaks poking up above the surface, sometimes in large groups, as they gulp air. The long, bony snout that puts the *longnose* in longnose gar is loaded with sharp teeth—and lots of them. The *bony* aspect of that beak is what I believe has kept the gar from becoming a truly beloved gamefish. They'll hit almost anything: bait, lures, spinners. The problem is, with very little flesh in the beak, there's nothing in which to set a hook. Lucky anglers (myself included) manage to land gar with traditional tackle, but I'd estimate the successful hookup rate at about 5% with normal gear. There's been much written (and posted on YouTube) about bait fishing for gar; but to successfully fish cut or live bait for longnose gar, you're likely talking about waiting for the fish to swallow the hook and bait. Though these fish can be cut off and released, I'm guessing the survival rate of such deeply hooked fish is dismal to zero. I know, *they're only gar,* but they've brought me many hours of fun. As with any fish or wildlife I pursue, I dislike the concept of waste, needless suffering and pointless death.

After days and weeks of research, I came upon the concept of the rope fly. As scientific fishing concepts go, it's rather silly in an ingenious sort of way. The rope fly just a frayed piece of nylon rope and the idea is that it tangles in the gars' myriad of teeth. The concept is so silly, but it works. Many gar anglers (and there *aren't* many) add hooks and beads and spinners and flashy dressings, but a plain-old six-inch piece of nylon rope, sufficiently frayed, will catch fish. It looks as much like a minnow, the gar's preferred prey, as anything else fishermen cast. The rope fly is big, weird and fluffy but, once slicked back under the surface of the water, it's close enough to a baitfish to fool gar—at least some of the time. It may be a French Impressionist's version of a baitfish, but a baitfish nonetheless.

The issue, for me anyway, was learning how to *not* set the hook. I know it's a ridiculous concept, especially because there *is no hook.* Still, with a lifetime of rearing back upon feeling or seeing the strike of a trout, pike or bass, it's a hard habit to break. Gar need to mouth the fly a bit, often thrashing back and forth in the water several times to fully entangle the fly in those plentiful teeth. Knowing when to finally apply pressure and raise the rod tip (and how *fast* to raise the rod tip) is the key to successful gar fishing. After two years of avid gar pursuit, I still strip the fly out of their mouth on a fairly frequent basis. It's hard to cure myself of the *set the hook!* programming, but I'm working on it; a lot, in fact, sometimes twice a week.

In May, June and July, the gar have a very agreeable habit of basking on the surface of the water together, often in groups of anywhere from a dozen to a hundred. They seem to like each other's company and this makes sight fishing a dream. There aren't many big fish that are conducive to sight fishing around here. Gar can be taken by blind casting when they are disagreeably sitting in the deeper water, but it is usually an exercise in frustration. From what I've experienced, they prefer their prey swimming right past their nose. I don't know if this is due to poor eyesight, or is rather an evolutionary example of economy of motion that they've developed over 100 million years. I've had gar chase a rope fly (and lures) from a fair distance, so I don't write them off as having poor eyesight as easily as some other observers have done. I think they just like their food to come to them as many predators, terrestrial and otherwise, do. I've observed small groups of gar herding schools of minnows into the shallows, working together. This is not typical large freshwater predator behavior. They seem to have an arsenal of tricks up their scaly sleeves.

When sight fishing, a gar day usually needs warmth (to keep them basking near the surface) and a calm surface with plenty of sunlight. I've been out many days when the water was slightly warmer than the air and even with bright sunlight, the gar were difficult. Lying on the bottom in twelve or fourteen feet of water, they'll shoot to the surface to grab flies or minnows, and disappear just as quickly. These are the most frustrating days of all because you can see the fish, but rarely have time to cast before they are gone again. Gar aren't particularly well camouflaged, but I've seen an entire pod of gar seemingly disappear when a cloud passes over, only to reappear with the sun. For these reasons, I always pick warm, calm, sunny days—the hotter the better. And, though many might tell you that gar fishing is best done at night, I find mid-afternoon on a sweltering day to be the perfect time.

When I finally started fishing for gar, I was told with some certainty that to chase them in a kayak was a fool's errand and likely to get me bit, cut by scales, punctured by sharp fins and/or capsized. I think death was mentioned as well. While I may be a fool, I'd handled large fish in the kayak plenty of times and didn't feel that the gar would be much different. In fact, there was only one way I did find gar to be difficult: They are very slimy. Though gloves aren't generally recommended for catch-and-release fishing, due to the possibility of damaging the delicate slime layer, they become a necessity when handling gar (in any sized boat). The slime layer of a gar is something to behold. It's thick, like mucous. Despite their scales, teeth and disposition, I think the gar's best defense against human fishermen is that slime. They're very hard to hang onto. It took several trips to consistently hook gar on rope flies, but it only took one trip to make me realize I needed to wear gloves while landing, handling and releasing them. A good day gar fishing usually ends with a healthy layer of slime on me, my clothes and my kayak. It's not for everyone, especially my laundress.

It had been a long morning at work. I'd had human-based frustrations, self-made frustrations, mechanical frustrations and some heartache on a personal level. I was ready to get out of there. It didn't help that all morning I kept glancing out the window at the tree outside my office. The sun was out. It was hot, and the wind was absent. Trying to be a responsible employee, I forced myself not to think about gar fishing. It worked for a while.

Once out of work and on the water, I only had a couple of boxes I wanted to check off. 1.) I wanted to catch some gar—preferably some *big* gar. 2.) I wanted to have some fun. The two things aren't mutually exclusive and I was fairly certain I could pull both off before the sun went down. The first gar of the day was a fair specimen, around thirty inches. Typical gar in this creek run from about two feet to about four. I've seen some babies, but rarely. I've also seen some five-footers, but not very often. The larger fish tend to be grayish colored females, adorned with spots on their tails and ray-like fins. In bright mid-day, the big girls almost glow blue. The males are generally smaller, yellow and green and spotted over the length of their entire bodies.

Giving the fish a moment or two to fully entangle its mouth in the rope fly, I watched him. He'd struck the lure only a few feet from the boat, which is very typical. When it seemed like the gar was well connected to my lure, I put the pressure on and hauled him toward the starboard side of the kayak. Donning my gloves as I did so, I reeled slowly. Upon seeing the kayak, the gar bolted for open water. I've read quite a bit about gar not being good fighters, but haven't found that to be the case. Like a large pike or muskie, the bigger ones will often play possum until they see the boat. More disconcertingly, they'll often wait until they're in the boat and then let loose. In this regard, I suppose that the small kayak might not be the ideal place to deal with the antics of a large fish but—then again—that's a part of why I do it. *Adventure fishing* someone in the business might call it. I just call it checking off Box Number Two: Having Some Fun. To date, I've landed a lot of gar, and some very big ones. I've dropped a couple in the boat, but they've all flipped harmlessly out of the kayak mostly because there's nowhere else to go. Occasionally I've really fumbled the fish and they've gone overboard before I could untangle the rope lure from their teeth. Aside from almost losing a brand new rod one afternoon, this hasn't proven too difficult, since they can be brought back in for another try as long as they're still connected—and with rope flies and sturdy line, they almost always are. Once they're hooked, they're hooked—even without a hook. On a few occasions smaller gar, which are excessively acrobatic and combative, have landed in my lap. No injuries (to me or the gar) though, I've learned to carry an extra pair of shorts; because once you're slimed, you're slimed. Despite all the warnings I received about battling gar in a kayak, I've never gotten injured.

The fish retreated at the sight of the kayak and pulled me in a half-circle. I brought the gar in again. My technique for landing gar is one I read about from another kayak gar fisherman (I think there's only two of us). Much like lipping a bass, gar can be brought under control by grabbing them around the snout and lifting them quickly from the water. The technique subdues them very quickly. I suppose if I was being lifted "airward" by my nose, I'd be subdued rather easily as well. Though the technique isn't without problems, it works almost every time. The most important part in pulling it off successfully is a firm grip. A *very firm grip*. The gars' slime layer extends well down to the end of that slimy, toothy, cartoon-character beak, and if you don't get the grip right, you'll suddenly have those rows of teeth sliding backward through your hand. It's a bit like a hacksaw, I guess. In reality it's *just like* a hacksaw, only the blades are bigger.

Pulling my gloves tight, I raised the gar's nose above the water and made a grab for him. *Got him*. For the size, I initially thought it was a big female. It turned out to be a *very big* male. Still considerably smaller than the females, he was one of the better males I've ever landed. Deeply spotted down his back and sides, he was a beautiful specimen as slimy dino-fish go.

The two most difficult parts of handling and releasing rope-fly gar are first, letting go of the beak, and secondly, getting the fly untangled from those teeth. Gar—even once in the kayak—are pretty docile as long as you have them by the nose. When you let go (which becomes a necessity very quickly), all bets are off. Sometimes they stay quietly in your lap or at your feet while you begin the often-laborious process of removing the fly from their teeth. Each strand has to be removed so as to ensure the fish doesn't starve to death once released with its mouth permanently bound shut.

Once the gar was in the boat I moved quickly, pausing only once to turn on the time-lapse GoPro camera for some photos. Prying the big male's jaws open, I was relieved to see that he was only caught by a few strands. I was surprised that he'd even stayed attached. Once freed of the lure, he posed with me for a photo or two before I released him back over the side. In return for my trouble, he gave me a lap full of water with a powerful flick of his tail before disappearing into the murky water.

I'd spotted the male in a pod of six gar. After the disturbance of his fight, the others were nowhere to be seen. For all their toughness, longnose gar won't tolerate a lot of disturbance. This is part of why I feel kayak fishing for gar is so productive. It's very quiet. Too much casting from me or violent thrashing from one of their number who's been hooked will put them down, often for an hour or more. Sometimes they submerge. Other times, and more commonly, they'll simply move off and resurface somewhere else on the creek. After releasing the gar and washing the slime off of my gloves, I paddled around the familiar water, pausing only to watch a bald eagle pass overhead with a fish in its talons, eventually lighting in a tall pine tree to eat. The gar were nowhere to be found. Most of my successes on gar have come from a half-dozen places, all within twenty minutes paddling of one other. I was hoping for big gar and there is one place in particular where the big females tend to hang together in fairly large numbers. I paddled out toward Lake Ontario and the Yacht Club. I prefer, of course, the more secluded upper reaches of this particular creek, but I was there to catch gar and check off those boxes and it always seemed to be the quiet water near the Yacht Club that held the biggest gar in the largest numbers.

I'd only just put my paddle down when I spotted a gang of at least thirty gar lounging near the bank of the creek opposite the huge sailboats and luxury yachts. On the first cast, I dragged the fly in front of the nose of the biggest female gar I could see, and she struck violently. I jumped, shocked, and pulled it right out of her mouth. Gar were lying everywhere on the surface. What had seemed to be thirty fish was actually closer to a hundred and thirty. They were all around me. Every now and then a back or a beak would break the surface, leaving a distinctive oval ripple in the water that is quite unlike that left by a trout or a bass. I placed the fly carefully in front of another large female, only ten feet from the kayak. She struck and I once again ripped the rope lure right out of her mouth. With all the fish around me—perhaps more than I've ever seen in one place—I was wired and jumpy as hell.

Calm down, I chided myself.

The next gar to which I cast was a true giant. Well over fifty-inches long, it was far and away the biggest of all the fish around me. Carefully opening the bail on the reel I aimed and placed the fly about six feet in front of her, bringing it slowly and deliberately past her nose. She twitched and I tensed, but before she could grab the fly, a very small male gar shot out in front of her and was off with it. I tried pulling quickly to dislodge him from the fly before he got too tangled, but he—of course— was hooked very well. Once I'd released him, I set about searching for the giant female. She was gone.

Though I landed four or five fish, a couple of them respectable thirty-six inchers, the fishing for the first two hours wasn't spectacular. I could check off Box 1 because I caught fish, but didn't quite yet have enough fun to check off Box 2. In between fish, I was distracted. When you fish to distract yourself, is there any hope when you're distracted from fishing? Truth be told, one of the main reasons I made the long drive to Oak Orchard Creek to spend time in the company of my beloved slime-fish is that I had other boxes to check off earlier in the day. It was the final day for Benefits Enrollment at my day job. I had to go through my list of benefits and check off every box and make my selections. Life Insurance. Health Insurance. Dental Insurance. Vision. And then ditto for my spouse and my dependents. Jennifer was the only dependent I had left on my insurance, and I had to remove her from every entry, and give a reason. They had her listed under every section as Jennifer Spring, 24. Jennifer Spring never made 24. To make matters worse, I had to give a reason. What do you say? I said simply "death". Each and every time. *Death. Death. Death. Death.* It was brutal. Eight months after burying my kid and buying her headstone, I got the gentle corporate reminder to make sure that I permanently removed her from my benefits. It's not that I don't think of her every day. It's not that I don't think about her death every day. I just wish they hadn't made me check off those boxes to ensure it was permanent and that my records were correct. I understand the concept and the necessity, but it didn't lessen my desire to throw my computer through my office window. Instead, I went fishing. That is my answer to many things these days. I guess it always has been.

At some point around 3 p.m. the fish started hitting in earnest. The group of 100-plus fish grew larger and more active. They were splashing all around me and my nerves were fraying, though in a good way. If I had my office computer with me, I likely wouldn't have tossed it out of the kayak. It's more art than science, but waiting for the opportunity to cast at a *good* fish is difficult when there are a bunch of *pretty good* fish all around you. I was as patient as I could be. Before long, I was up to ten fish in the boat, and at least hooking up on every other cast. Some of them were big. One was a four-footer, which was a handful, pulling the kayak around in circles before coming in for his close-up.

The next hour was mayhem. You hear people joking about being tired from reeling in fish. I actually got arm fatigue from casting and reeling in fish. Talk about your first-world problems. Targeting only the bigger specimens, I had a good run of forty-inchers. I'm guessing by the time I hooked the last fish, I'd landed twenty of them and probably connected with another ten that never got to the boat through their stubbornness or my failures. Checking my watch, I realized I'd been on the water about four hours. It was an hour drive to home, and I'd caught more gar in one afternoon than I'd ever dreamt of. It was probably time to quit. I weighed the possibility that I could conceivably be home in time for dinner.

Spotting a bruiser of a female gar on my way back up the creek, I could not resist a cast or two. Though she wasn't in a larger pod, two smaller males hovered behind her, as is often the case, although their breeding season should have been over by now. I've found in the last couple years that sometimes fish that *aren't* with a larger group are easier to target and more likely provoked into a strike. It's counterintuitive. I would think that in a larger group, the competition for food would be higher and the strikes more frequent, but have found the opposite to be true. Show me a large, lone gar and I can almost guarantee the fish will, at the very least, follow the lure to the boat. Very often, solitary gar are responsible for the most viscous strikes.

I dropped the lure well past the trio of fish, let it sink a bit, and then began an erratic retrieve alongside the snout of the very large female. Praying she'd snatch it before the two small, pesky males behind her had a chance, I saw the telltale twitch of her position.

Don't blow it, Spring. Don't blow it!

She grabbed the fly with a lightning-fast twitch to the side, her body transforming from a straight line to a snake-like *S* in less than a blink of the eye. Several yards from the kayak, I could clearly see her mouthing the rope fly, its whiteness radiating through the blue-green murk of the creek. When she began shaking her head from side to side, like a dog shaking a bath-towel, I raised the spinning rod ever so slightly. There was pressure there. After a count of three, I gently raised the tip up. The fish, realizing this minnow wasn't necessarily a minnow, headed for the bottom of the creek. Gar don't usually do that, preferring to fight it out at the top of the water column in a splashing brawl. She went straight under the kayak and stopped.

Well this is a new one.

Glancing at my small fish finder, I could see her outline. Not on the bottom of the fourteen-foot depth, she was about half way down. Risking a glance over the edge, I couldn't see more than a foot into the murk. But, raising the rod tip just a bit farther, I could feel her down there. She didn't pull back. I quickly checked the drag on my reel, and decided that I didn't want to sit there all afternoon. More importantly, I *wanted that fish!*

I reeled slowly at first, then more quickly, dredging her steadily toward the surface and the kayak. Reaching forward for a moment, I switched on the camera. If things went to hell, I wanted it documented. For a moment, I thought I'd traded the gar for a cinderblock, but then inch-by-inch she came into view. All of four feet, she was perfectly docile at the side of the kayak. Perhaps her initial run and dive had worn her out. *Perhaps.* For the umpteenth time that afternoon, I slipped on my fishing gloves and prepared myself for the unexpected.

Taking a deep breath, I lifted the rod tip and her snout cleared the water. I made a grab for her. My left forearm strained against the weight and my normally very stable kayak rocked on its keel. This was a big fish. Not *the* longest of the year, but at least Number Two. In girth, and probably in weight, she may have been the biggest.

Lifting her from the water, I had her by the beak in one hand, cradling her carefully under the belly with my other. Only a second into the operation, I clearly saw that her teeth had barely tangled in the fly. That she stayed on this long was nothing short of miraculous. (I think the larger fish, with their larger teeth often are harder to hook because of this. The smaller gar's teeth—while sharp—have more of a Velcro-like property and get tangled in everything from flies, to nets and t-shirts). At four-feet, she was too big to lay solidly in my lap, so I carefully laid her lengthwise in the kayak with her snout in my direction. Quickly prying her mouth open with my left hand, I reached in with my right to free her teeth of the several strands of nylon. Like many of the larger fish I've handled, she was calm. I wanted a photo of her, remembering the camera had been going the whole time. Planning the move carefully, I hoisted the big female gar for the camera and watched the LED blink twice. *Good enough.*

Preparing to release the big gar—and quite pleased with myself, I must add—I leaned left and put her snout over the left side of the boat. Gar, being quite comfortable breathing air, don't require reviving. I typically just let the big ones slip over the side of the kayak and back into the drink. Sliding like a slimy python through my left hand, she was on her way back to her home creek when she suddenly slashed sideways.

The move was not unlike when she struck the fly: Lightning fast. The end result wasn't a lap full of water and a laugh this time, however. I suddenly had a lap full of gar. I instinctively recoiled and shoved the huge, fat fish off my lap. In other similar instances, the fish has ultimately flipped out of the boat and I was left laughing and perhaps a little wet. This gar, however, flipped down past the foot pegs in the kayak and was suddenly thrashing around on top of the fish finder. I wasn't laughing.

When her tail caught under my spinning rod (my *lucky gar rod* no less), she sent it flying into the water. *That looked intentional!* I managed to catch it with the paddle before it sunk out of sight. When I returned my attention to the big, vengeful gar, it wasn't difficult to find her. Sometime in the mayhem—I assume when she took a gulp for air—she'd opened that cartoon dinosaur beak and closed it over my ankle. I ditched both gloves for a better grip and pried her mouth off my leg. The needle-like teeth cut into my fingers. With teeth in the back of my ankle and teeth in the front of my ankle, it was like being in the grip of an alligator. As soon as I leveraged myself (her/myself, *whomever*) free, I tossed her very unceremoniously over the edge of the kayak. Unlike every other gar I've ever released, she did not dive for the bottom. She hung next to the kayak, as if thinking *I wonder if I could jump back in there.*

Thankfully, she didn't.

The kayak was trashed. My tools were scattered all over the deck. Monofilament line was tangled around everything. The fish-finder was bathed in slime and I was soaked. I washed my hands in the creek, and began straightening things up for the paddle back to the launch. The trickle of blood down my leg didn't concern me. I hoped my own bodily fluids were washing some of the Toxic Avenger slime and whatever nastiness it might carry out of my wound. Feeling some pain on the back of my leg as well, I reached behind my ankle and came up with a thick smear of blood. I'm not sure *how* much the back of my ankle was bleeding, because the hand I checked it with was bleeding as well. At some point, I started laughing at the absurdity of catching these toothy, slimy, ancient survivors in a small kayak. I wouldn't trade it for all of the steelhead in Washington State or all the brown trout in the Beaverkill.

Mission accomplished. The fun box had been checked.

The Flood

The summer of 2017 Lake Ontario flood was not a thousand or even a one hundred-year event, but it was still something very few had ever witnessed, and none in recent memory. A naturalist at heart, I pondered this flood, especially how it affected the fishing. A selfish matter to ponder, to be sure, in the midst of a natural disaster, but the thing is, I never really considered it a disaster. Lake Ontario was once a *whole lot* higher, covering the Niagara Frontier—the entire area I now call home— with twenty or thirty feet of water, consequently this flood was just a blip on the ten-thousand year radar. We're so wrapped up in predictions and what is supposed to be normal that people sometimes lose sight of the fluctuating nature of Nature. Everything comes in cycles: high and low; drought and flood; feast and famine; overpopulation and extinction. Most natural phenomenon follow these patterns, and Lake Ontario, for all its greatness, isn't exempt.

The local (and sometimes national) news coverage of the beach erosion showed sandbags around homes, and some of them on my home water were featured prominently. None were destroyed, though dozens suffered water damage while many yards of beachfront and several overhanging decks were lost to the violent erosion. I spent an afternoon during one of the windier days at Golden Hill State Park, a few miles down the Lake from my hometown. The inland sea was angry that day, my friend. I watched clumps of sod dropping into the lake as eight and ten-foot waves battered the shore. It was nature at its damaging finest. I often joke with my Florida friends about their curious decision to live in the path of inevitable hurricanes just to escape a little snow. The 2017 Lake Ontario flood was probably the closest thing to that type of damage we'll ever see in Western New York.

The cause of the flood varies depending on whom you ask. There's a select number of people who blame the authorities who operate the enormous Moses-Saunders Dam. The dam spans the Saint Lawrence River from New York to Canada. Designed as a hydroelectric generation facility, it is a monstrous feat of engineering. Its secondary function is to serve as a level control for Lake Ontario. Consider that responsibility: *Controlling the level of a Great Lake.* The lake itself is over 7,300 square miles and 800 feet deep. That's a lot of water for one dam to control. What could possibly go wrong? In addition to whatever decisions were or were not made as far as water release from the Moses-Saunders in the early days of the flood, there were other factors. Rain at *my* end of the lake was relentless for weeks. Streams and rivers flooded and emptied their muddy contents into the lake. That additional water, combined with an equally relentless north wind, battered the shores of Lake Ontario as well as the inner tributaries. Releasing additional water from the Moses-Saunders finally took place, but only after the downstream areas of Quebec that had suffered their *own* flooding had dried out enough to accept the water. The eventual release of water caused ships in the Saint Lawrence (the river is a major shipping route from the Great Lakes to the Atlantic Ocean) to experience strong currents and dangerous navigational conditions for weeks after. The levels in the lake began receding. While the local news stations spouted off statistics about "Four Olympic-sized swimming pools going over the dam every second", the lake itself dropped very slowly over the course of the next months. In late September of 2017, things had only just returned to normal.

None of this, of course, kept me from fishing. As a result of the flood,

I caught fish in places where years prior there wasn't even any water. The fish took advantage of the high water and spread out into woodlands and fields along the creek, probably depositing eggs and little fish in places that hadn't seen them since 1952. I'm sure some of the small ponds along the creek had their populations bolstered by the adventurous fish. I pondered these things many days during the flood while playing amateur biologist and decided the high water was likely very good for most of the fish species. My friend and local outdoor columnist, Bill Hilts, Jr., reported the best fishing seen in the area in at least ten years. For the ancient species like my longnose gar and bowfin, I'm sure the Great Flood of 2017 elicited little more than a bored yawn.

Both Twelve-Mile Creek and Oak Orchard Creek were accessible. Pretty much *anything* is accessible with a kayak, even during flood stages. Some of the other creeks remained muddy into the summer, but those two cleared up relatively quickly. Another part of my natural history observation led me to conclude that the high levels and heavy currents from weeks prior likely scoured out some of the sediment that had settled into the creeks since their last good rinse in 1952. This could be a win-win, as the gravel would be more user-friendly for the spawning salmonids and native fish alike. While I continued to ponder the flood's impact on the local fishery, I quite congratulated myself on my deep thoughts and conclusions. *I love being a student of nature*, I thought, perhaps a little cockily. It happens.

Pulling up to the small marina, I could clearly see from the road above that the launch was once again accessible and only a foot or so higher than its normal level. *Progress,* I thought. Many of the docks submerged only a few weeks ago were emerging from the water. Coated in weeds, mud and an extraordinary number of northern water snakes, they weren't pretty but at least they were intact. Maneuvering down the driveway to the launch, I rounded a bend and the sight that met my eyes made me hit the brakes. The small marina-shop that once sold baitfish and licenses, drinks and tackle, was reduced to a pile of broken lumber. The sign that once hung above the door was propped against a portable toilet. The owner who told me early in the season that the floor had flooded and they were temporarily taking the business uphill was working an excavator, methodically lifting the pile of debris into two large, red, roll-off boxes.

As I unloaded the kayak onto the launch, only scant yards from the demolition, the owner's wife walked down the driveway with a small cooler in her hand. He jumped out of the excavator to meet her. They sat at a bench that was underwater on my last visit. Hugging and drinking beer together, they wore deep sadness on their faces. I'd seen them both enough over the years that I didn't want to ignore them, nor did I want to intrude on their moment. Still, I thought of my own isolation and sadness. If I were them, I'd wish I would say *something*.

"I didn't know you were going to tear it down," I offered.

"Had to. It was ruined." He had tears in his eyes. His wife put her arm around him again.

"End of an era," she said.

"I'm really sorry. I don't know what to say."

They seemed to appreciate that. She offered me a beer. Again, I didn't know what to say. Accept? Don't? Following my instincts (which include beer), I politely declined, but sat there with them for a few moments. The chitchat moved on from the depressing scene at hand. A bit later, after enjoying their company more than I might have guessed, I pushed the kayak out into the water and turned my face to the sun. My flippancy about the flood disappeared into that pile of what had once been a beloved family business.

I pondered a lot of things while fishing that afternoon. The fishing wasn't very good, and my mind wandered—always a dangerous proposition these days. Like many bad afternoons fishing when the distraction isn't enough, most of the things I pondered were sadness and unfairness and bitterness. I thought about the marina owners and their loss, and found it was good for once not to be thinking only of my own grief.

The Insecure Angler

*Each one of us requires the spur of insecurity
to force us to do our best.*
— Harold W. Dodds

The main reason I rarely fish competitively is insecurity. I've never been eager to please everyone. Ask my family, if you must, and please tell them I said hello! My predilections toward fishing have from early in my life always revolved around the peacefulness, the solitude and the communication and interaction with nature. I never saw the point of making a contest of it. I especially abhorred (and abhor) the presence of money, which, as I think is pretty well proven in the course of humanity, tends to always bring out the worst in *everyone*. Having a friendly one-on-one competition with a trusted fishing partner is one thing, but competing against dozens of other fishermen for cash prizes is quite another. No thank you. Part of that may be that I don't trust *myself* not to be overly competitive given the prizes and prestige that may be had by landing the biggest, heaviest, longest or *most* fish. Some of my close friends live for the competition. I never have. In that regard, it's probably *me* that is weird and/or defective. I assume that's the case. Did you read the title of this chapter? I'm a bit insecure.

One of my earliest competitive failures (I'm not going to list them all, so you can relax) involved a chunky brown trout caught in

Wilson-Tuscarora Harbor, the East Branch of my beloved Twelve-Mile Creek. One of the less well-known fishing derbies (I know, they call them *tournaments* now) had a kid-friendly entry fee, and my best friend and I entered. About fourteen years old and still too young to drive, we bummed a ride from Frank's dad to the harbor. Armed with a few fishing rods, our long minnow net and a bait pail, we trudged out onto the boat slips and set about the business at which we were well versed. Before daylight, we netted minnows gathered in the glow of the public boat launch's orange sodium lamps. After we secured several dozen and dumped them into the old bucket, we rigged our rods in the growing daylight and began fishing. With competition from stream fishermen, other shore fisherman, and the dozens of fishing boats out on the open water, the chance of two kids catching the winning fish was slim. We'd probably be fishing anyway and, for the few-dollar entry fee, we had nothing to lose. Munching on chocolate chip cookies and Pepsi, we watched our bobbers, carefully positioned in the shadows of the boat slips. For weeks, we'd caught a mix of rock bass and crappie, but also the occasional rainbow or brown trout. I didn't realize yet at that age what a blessing living on a Lake Ontario tributary was for fishing opportunities. Landing a good-sized rainbow only three days prior, it got me thinking about the competition. *Why not?*

After a dozen or so rock bass and the need to replenish our minnow supply and momentarily interrupt our fishing, the mid-morning slump occurred. Boredom ensued, and talked turned away from fish and toward high-school things like being a band-nerd, girls, working on the farm this upcoming summer and a thousand other things that seem important when you're fourteen. One of my bobbers was making lazy circles and I assumed it was just an unusually robust minnow trying to figure a way out of its unfortunate circumstance. Transfixed, if only because it soothed my boredom for a bit, I noticed the bobber heading more purposefully in one direction. I casually reached for the rod and was immediately thankful I had done so. It nearly slid off the wooden boat slip before I had my hand around it. The bobber was gone and I reared back on the rod, probably much harder than I should have.

Fish on!

The trout came in easily. It didn't fight much harder than the larger of the rock bass we'd landed already that morning, perhaps less so. Frank used the long-handled minnow net (we didn't know any better!) to land the fish for me. It was a pretty male brown trout, with yellow sides and vivid black and brown markings. Frank measured it.

"Sixteen."

"Fifteen is legal."

We discussed it. Competing with the big water boats, it wasn't unrealistic to think that a contest-placing brown trout might be upwards of twenty-five or even thirty inches. This, though a nice fat trout, by Lake Ontario standards it was just a baby. Had this been caught on a Catskill creek we'd have been thrilled, but it hadn't. One of us made the executive decision to release the fish, since it didn't have a prayer of placing in the derby. The derby ended at one that afternoon. Can you guess how large the winning fish was? I'll give you a moment. Fifteen inches? Sixteen? No. *No brown trout were entered.* That's right. We would have won in the brown trout category. I've remembered that story for forty years. You might think that it stands out in my memory because it's such an unusual thing.

I wish that were the case.

Not many months later, in the hot humid days of summer, we landed our first bowfin in Twelve-Mile. Scared to death of the eel-like monstrosity flopping around in the very small canoe, one of us pinned it down while the other measured it. As quickly as we could, we tag-teamed the slimy giant and tossed it back over the side of the canoe. In the days before the Internet, it took a bit of investigating to finally realize what we'd landed. It was a bowfin, the fish that would go on to become one of my favorites later in life. When I found a book on the conservation department's game-fish records at our local library, I found the most recent state-record was a twelve-pound fish. No expert fisherman at that point in my life, I thought that our fish must have been fourteen or fifteen pounds. Of course, something always seems bigger when it's flopping around your canoe and trying to bite you, but I had the measurement. It was a thirty-seven inch fish. I didn't know what that meant in weight, but it sure *seemed* bigger than twelve pounds. Just a few years ago I discovered a weight-length conversion chart for bowfin. A thirty-seven incher (if it is of average girth) is about a sixteen-pound fish. Even if it was skinnier than I remember, still fourteen or fifteen pounds. We could have shattered the state bowfin record—as kids!

We didn't.

As I became a more experienced fisherman, I moved away from the warm water species and entered into the enlightened world of fly rod trout fishing. I grew infatuated with mountain streams and matching the hatch. I never quite became a snob, but I was very much addicted. In the midst of my trout pursuits, my brother-in-law Steve needed a partner for a bass tournament on one of New York's Finger Lakes. I don't remember which lake it was, but I remember the contest. It was a sunny, windy and relatively fish-free day. Our boat in particular had *zero* keepers in the first few hours. I'd grown bored, whipping my bait-caster frantically until my arms were ready to give out. I daydreamed of my light fly rod and gossamer tippets, crystal flowing waters and beautiful native trout.

That's when the bass slammed my spinnerbait.

"Finally!" Steve yelled.

Suspended over a barely perceptible hump in the featureless depth, the bass hit with a ferocity that rivaled any I've ever caught. Here's the thing though: *I didn't catch him.* The bass made two spectacular jumps ten yards from the side of the boat. Though I was out of practice with my heavy bass gear, I knew how much I could pressure him and how much the line would take. I was careful, knowing this was potentially a cash fish. He looked to be every bit of five pounds; outstanding for this water.

It wasn't my lack of experience that did me in, but rather my lack of recent practice. You wouldn't think reeling in a fish would be (in Steve's words) a *perishable skill,* but apparently it is. I clumsily let my thumb drift over and onto the spool. Realizing my mistake as the bass pulled harder and the drag did not give, I removed my thumb far too quickly and gave the fish slack line for just a second. He took the opportunity to detach himself from the single hook and he was gone.

"What happened?!"

"I don't know!"

It was a quiet ride back to the weigh-in.

A few weeks back I was invited to join Scott, one of my friends and an avid salmon fisherman, for an early morning outing on Lake Ontario. No kayaks this time, but a real boat, downriggers, electronics and the knowledge of an experienced salmon-chaser. Deep water trolling isn't my area of expertise (read = I know nothing about deep water trolling) and I listened intently as Scott directed me what to do and how to help him set the lines. I started off on an insecure footing, simply because I didn't know anything about this type of fishing. I've been out trolling the Big Lake many times, but had never been asked to assist. It's all quite confusing, really. One of Scott's gifts is that he truly delights in taking inexperienced people out with him and *teaching.* It's something we have in common, and I appreciate that about him.

After an hour or so we'd landed one small salmon. Any salmon is a delight to fight on rod and reel, though this was perhaps *the* smallest I'd ever seen. It came in without much trouble at all. The second fish, a few moments later, was a bruiser. Line sang off the level-wind reel. Scott tried to hand me the rod, obviously excited it was a big fish.

"First big fish goes to the guest. That's my rule!"

I insisted insistently that he land the fish. I really didn't mind, realizing trolling is a team sport and whether or not you happen to be the fisherman who gets the fish is as much a matter of luck as anything else. Scott fought the big salmon like a pro. The give-and-take of line was exhilarating to behold. I suddenly realized that, in another life, this kind of fishing might be something I'd like to learn. The salmon came to the boat twice, and each time more lined screamed off the reel in protest as the fish recognized the danger of the boat. The third time, Scott asked me to get the net.

"Wait for my signal," he advised.

I may not be a big water devotee, but I know how to net and land fish.

"Now," he said, as the big male king rolled alongside the boat. Scott lifted his rod tip as I slid the net expertly under the huge salmon. What happened next was not my fault. I wanted to yell, *"It's not my fault, not my fault!"* The treble hook from the lure caught on the leading edge of the net. In a single, leveraged flip, the salmon was out of the net before he was ever in it, and gone.

"What happened?!"

That phrase again. I flashed back twenty years to the lost bass, the released trout and the record-smashing bowfin.

"Hook caught on the net."

"You probably had the net too high, then."

"Sorry..."

"The guest always gets the first big fish in my boat. We should have done that."

I'd insisted on breaking Scott's rule in his own boat. The netting disaster might have been an error in calculation, but the rule violation was my own doing. There wasn't much to say. I apologized. Scott isn't the type to hold grudges, but that was a twenty-pound salmon, maybe more. You don't get one every day.

Gone.

"At least we weren't fishing for money!" Scott said, feigning cheeriness through teeth that may have been gritted.

Oh, I could have screwed that up too, I thought, shuddering at the thought of losing a big-dollar fish.

While I've had great days on the water with my fishing partners, I also realize the joy of being alone. There's far less expected of me when I set my own expectations. And, trust me on this, I don't set expectations for myself very high. I still manage to disappoint myself, but nowhere near as frequently as I seem to disappoint my fishing partners.

My current fishing partners are an interesting mix. Though we don't fish together very often, Randy and I do share the water occasionally for an afternoon of bass fishing. He's a kayak fishing expert and a very good tournament bass fisherman. I find myself fishing my *ass* off every time we head out to fish together. I have no desire to show him up. I just don't want to *be* shown up. It's not a desirable trait, nor one I'm particularly proud that I've adopted. I have screwed up so many times with so many experienced fishermen, that I just want *one* fishing partner to whom I can at least feel equal. I don't feel equal to Randy, but I try hard!

My other fishing partners these days, including Joy, are a bit less experienced than I. That seems to be a good fit. It works for me. I can be the *better* fisherman while still being not-so-great. I frequently welcome the inexperienced fisherman into my fishing fold. In fact, if you're not very good and don't know what you're doing, give me a call. I'd be happy to take you out!

A few weeks ago I fished once more for longnose gar. Again, the gar fishing was spectacular. Again, over twenty fish—many of them forty-plus inches—came to the kayak. In my element, I felt like I knew what I was doing and wished someone had been there to see it. At sunset, I paddled the kayak up the launch ramp and unloaded my gear. The owner strolled down the hill from his house.

"How'd you do?"

"Well, I was gar fishing, and got somewhere around twenty."

"Wow, twenty gar. Really? *Gar*?"

"Yeah, I know. Sounds crazy."

"No, no. If you're going for gar, and you got twenty gar, that's a *great day!*"

Appreciating the enthusiasm, I wondered if he was a fisherman. The answer was likely *yes,* given the nature of his business. I then wondered if he was any good. If he wasn't very good, I could always use a new fishing partner.

Ancient Aliens

My love affair with Twelve-Mile Creek, such as it is, is an enduring one. Of the fifty years I've spent here on our little blue planet, at least forty-five of them have been spent fishing on my home creek. You know I have a (perhaps unhealthy or poorly thought out) fond affinity for the longnose gar—one of our most ancient fishes. If you've been paying attention (and I sincerely hope that you have), you'll note that my home water contains no gar. In order to catch those slimy, toothy survivors of the dinosaur era, I need to drive an hour east. Oh, there are some gar in the upper stretches of the lower Niagara River, but the Niagara River isn't well suited to my kind of kayak fishing. Most places on the river where the gar are plentiful require a good boat and a better motor in order to stay on the dry side of the river. All of my kayak-based gar fishing has taken place on Oak Orchard Creek. It's home to big water snakes, bowfin, carp, and very few human beings. I don't mind the drive. It helps me clear my head and my head is increasingly less clear these days. One Friday afternoon, after a particularly long and stressful day at work and one in which the nightmare imagery of Jen's death invaded my brain more persistently than it had in recent memory, I took off to my home water.

The July heat beat down, shimmering off the calm surface. I wished I'd had the energy to drive out to Oak Orchard. It was a perfect gar day.

Still, my goal was distraction and some bass or pike or both would fit the bill just fine. On the way in, I paused by an old familiar tangle of fallen trees and pulled a nice largemouth bass out. A few moment's later, a small northern pike took the lure. Small? Sorry, *ridiculously small.* He may have been a new personal best for me as far as *small pike* go. Looking both in size and coloration like a hot-dog gone bad, I still couldn't believe he could get his mouth around the big crankbait, much less suck it in as far as he did.

Farther on up, within sight of my destination, I paused to cast along the deep edge of some lily pads. Just as I was about to release the first cast, a dark shadow caught my eye. While not exceptionally common, muskies are not unheard of in my home creek. It looked for certainty like a big muskie. I back-paddled quickly to pause the boat and selected a different rod. Dropping my lucky spinnerbait rig several feet in front of the long shadow, I brought it past its nose. Not surprisingly, the presentation was met with indifference. It was hot, and I was not surprised the fish might be relatively inactive. Still, hot weather is not exactly prime muskie conditions. I've seen them and their northern pike cousins basking earlier in the season when warmth was more at a premium, but this seemed odd, something I'd expect from a gar. Thing is, though, there are no longnose gar in Twelve-Mile Creek. I cast again, this time with the crankbait. A slight twitch in the long shadow suddenly turned into a savage s-shape as the fish grabbed the lure. I set the hook. The lure promptly flew over my head after only the briefest resistance. The fish returned to its basking spot, seemingly not spooked at all. With the two large treble hooks on the crankbait, there's no reason that fish wasn't hooked. Red flags started going up: It didn't chase, but hit when the lure was perpendicular to its head; and even with a hard hit, it didn't hook up. It didn't disappear after the failed hit, unlike any pike or muskie I've ever known. If I didn't know better, I'd say that fish was a gar. But…but…there *are no longnose gar on Twelve-Mile Creek.* I've fished here my whole life. I pay *attention* to these things. Close attention!

I paddled closer. As I neared the fish, now only ten yards away, it became apparent. It was a big, blue, female gar. A first. I didn't bother looking through my tackle for a gar fly. The gar-box was at home. While this knowledge set in, I noticed the two smaller males finning quietly behind her, waiting for their chance to fertilize her eggs. I pondered this for a bit. Was I the first person to ever see gar here? Should I tell anyone? I supposed it didn't matter, since no one really fished for gar around here anyway. Pleased with my discovery, I watched the fish a while longer.

Something of a natural historian, I thought over the gar sighting thoroughly as the afternoon wound down and I paddled back toward the lake and the launch. With ideal, sunny, calm conditions, I also kept a wary eye out for more gar. It wasn't long before I spotted another pair. Both of them were small males, located a half-mile from the original three.

Twelve-Mile Creek has gar!

When fishing for gar, I'm usually looking for pods of a dozen or more fish, so five gar isn't exactly a bonanza. However, in water that hasn't traditionally held gar it was an exciting concept to contemplate. Maybe the high water earlier in the season distributed the fish into places they wouldn't normally be? I discounted the idea. These fish have existed in this watershed for tens of millions of years, seeing the coming and going of the ice ages and major fluctuations in water levels that would make this year's two or three foot flood seem like an afternoon sprinkle. I guessed that the fish had always been there, at least in some numbers, on and off over the years. My census was not a scientific one, but I learned enough in college to know one female fish that can lay thousands of eggs, along with a bunch of males eager to fertilize them, could make for a healthy gar colony in a short amount of time. Twelve-Mile Creek is small water compared to Oak Orchard, but the bait is plentiful and there are holding pools—such as the gear-eating Cow Bridge—deep enough for those fish to winter over.

I'm not a mathematician, nor a fisheries biologist, but I'd wager that my hypothetical grandchildren may one day find Twelve-Mile Creek teeming with longnose gar. And I can only assume they'll say *why would anyone fish for those disgusting creatures?* I decided to keep the find to myself, for a while anyway.

It's good to have a secret, even if it's one that no one particularly cares about.

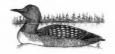

On an Island

Loneliness expresses the pain of being alone and
solitude expresses the glory of being alone.
—Paul Tillich

I've become a pretty good bass fisherman, mostly through trying to catch everything else. Perusing the preceding pages, you may think I have a distaste for bass, both of the large and smallmouth persuasion. It's not true. My first *real* trophy fish was a slammer of a largemouth bass (in retrospect, it was probably only about two pounds, but seemed huge back then) that inexplicably took a poorly cast Jitterbug under the hot noonday sun. Up until that point, I'd never experienced anything quite like the power of that hit, erupting from the lily pads like a submarine-launched ICBM. With an abundance of local pike and bowfin, my interest quickly swerved away from bass and toward the bigger, scarier fish. I did, however, spend a lot of time honing my fly-fishing skills on bass. They were much easier to come by in my hometown than trout. Back then, my trout fishing was limited to a yearly trip to the Catskills, and occasional forays into the southern hills of Western New York. I'm fairly sure that, in the early 80s, I was the only kid fishing with a fly rod for bass. I enjoyed it as practice and got pretty good at fooling even bigger bass with flies and poppers, but bass still didn't hold my interest compared to pike, pickerel and bowfin. I was a weird kid.

I like bass. I don't *love* them, but I respect bass when I'm not disrespecting them to poke at my bass-addict friends. Due to the fact that I throw a lot of large, heavy hardware in search of the toothier predators, I very often catch *very* big bass. If I land a big bass alone, I'll admire it and congratulate myself on a job well done. If I'm with a bass fishing friend, I'll snort in distaste and say something to the effect of: *"It's just a bass."* It makes me laugh every time and, after all, isn't that what's important?

I do like bass, but please don't let it get out. I have a reputation to maintain.

The afternoon was hot. I parked the kayak under the Lake Road bridge to enjoy the shade for a bit before continuing on up the creek. I'd been casting large spinnerbaits and crankbaits in hopes of a pike, but the water temperature soared in excess of 76 degrees. I knew, under the circumstances, the pike were likely out at the mouth, hanging at the fringes of cooler water near the deep lake until fall arrived. I cast the big hardware a few more times, but couldn't even entice a bowfin into a half-hearted follow. It was simply too hot for fishing. I had some free time, though, and wanted to be on the water. I figured I'd stay under the bridge and cast for an hour or two, waiting for the sun to disappear behind the trees, perhaps triggering the fish into a feeding pattern. My hopes weren't high. Sitting under the bridge, I was only a few yards from my after-school bass fly-casting hot spot. Back then, thirty-odd years ago, the stream bottom was easily navigable in my hip waders. Now entirely choked in weeds, the bottom was so soft I wouldn't dare set foot in it for fear of a slow, sucking death. I spent a few minutes pondering how different everything looked. The bridge and its cooing pigeons hadn't changed. They used to shit directly *on* me. These days, they just paint my kayak. I've learned where the perches are but sometimes neglect to avoid them. Glancing at the bank where I used to wade under the bridge, I could almost make out the ghost of my younger self in the shadows. Funny-looking kid he was. Long hair, white T-shirt, hip waders, cheap fly rod in hand.

What a weirdo.

What advice would I give him? I don't know. All things considered, I probably wouldn't want to change him very much. After the last few years though, I might warn him to keep a wary eye to the future because life can hit you hard. I don't know, though. I probably wouldn't tell him that. I wouldn't want to ruin his fishing.

A few moments in quiet contemplation brought me back around to things I didn't want to think about and images I didn't want to imagine. Busying myself (which is what it was all about), I shuffled through my tackle box, looking for something bassy. I settled on the Loon Lake Special. That's not really the name. The small, blue jointed Rapala provided us with more dinner-perch at Loon Lake the last few years than anything with which I've ever fished. Joy and I call it the Loon Lake Special. Bass like it too. I cast toward the ghost-kid and he didn't even glance my way, so engrossed was he in his fishing. The rod tip suddenly jerked downward and I was into a small bass, probably a descendant of all those fly rod bass I'd pulled from under the bridge. A second cast produced a second bass. For a few moments, the fishing provided the distraction I needed. After landing four small bass and a good-sized perch under the bridge, I decided to work up into the creek. There's a stretch of downed trees that usually produces some good bass and the occasional bowfin. With the spinning rod cradled in my lap, I paddled out of the shade and into the heat of the day.

I'm going bass fishing! I laughed. Come on you bass fishermen, laugh with me!

One savage strike resulted in a big largemouth. Actually it was a *very big* largemouth. I turned on the camera and posed with him for a photo. I take great delight in sending my bass fishing friends photos of me with *very big bass.* It always makes me laugh, picturing their reactions since they *know* for certain that's not what I was fishing for. Maybe this time I'll tell them that I *was* bass fishing. Maybe. No, probably not. What fun would that be? They wouldn't believe me anyway.

Another fish grabbed the Loon Lake Special as soon as it hit the water, and promptly tangled itself in some submerged branches. I'm not a fan of heavy line (even for heavy fish) and I was worried that trying to horse the bass out of the timber would result in a broken line and, worse, leaving the fish with a lure stuck in its maw. I paddled toward the sunken tree. In only two feet of water, I stepped out of the kayak. The bottom was firm enough, though weeds grabbed at my ankles. Reaching into the branches to untangle the line, I pulled vertically and the bass came up. Somehow, before I could lip him, he made another dive into the same spot, tangling the line this time around *two* branches. It took some maneuvering, stick snapping, and patience to bring him up this time. By the time it was done, I was wet. Wanting only to release the fish (though he was big enough to be photo-worthy), I noticed my kayak drifting away. There wasn't much current this late in the season, but it was pushed by the light breeze toward the center of the creek where it was certainly more than two feet deep. With the bass grasped in my right hand, I splashed through the water and snatched the kayak, soaking the bottom of my shorts. Somewhere in my lurch for the boat, I dropped the bass. Anyone watching from the bridge would have thought *what a weirdo*.

Indeed.

As soon as the midday bite had begun, it was over. I traversed the east and west banks of the creek, fishing each likely looking spot and (yes) hoping for a bass. But it was clearly over, at least for now. I contemplated parking under the bridge again where I could wait for the temperature to drop a bit, but the thoughts from which I'd been distracting myself flooded back. Some days, there isn't much of a break.

Images of the last year played in my mind. I can't explain them all to you or to anyone, but they are the stuff of nightmares. Jen hearing the news of her terminal illness. Jen having her seizures. Jen after a horrific surgery. Jen as she wept for the children she would never have. Jen's last words. Jen as she lay dying. I don't know how people survive this onslaught of black memory. Hell, I don't know how I've survived it. In my darker moments, the images of my daughter and what she endured play over and over in my mind. Sometimes, some days, people will be having the most mundane conversations with me about their cars or their bills, their indigestion or their ridiculous expectations and as they speak all I can picture is my dying daughter. I want to shake them sometimes and say, *really, that's all you've got?* Most days, I can pull on the mask of the guy I used to be and lend a compassionate ear. Other days, I want to slap them. I'm still that compassionate guy they expect, but I'm stretched a bit more thin these days and those dark moments come frequently, therefore I fish. I paused on the tributary time machine at no place in particular. For a moment, I wanted to paddle down to the bridge and tell young Joel to run like hell; run far, far away. I'm not sure he'd listen, and I'm not sure where he could go to escape his future.

A common occurrence for the grieving is to have feelings of isolation. This realization came not only from my research and reading, but also unfortunately from my personal experience after Jennifer's death. The weeks after the funeral were full of well-wishers, helpful friends and family. In a slow fade, though, people eventually began moving away. I know this is a well-documented phenomenon, but it seems to be even more prominent when the death of a child (even an adult child) is involved. People don't want to be reminded that *their* child could die, too. Who *would* want to be reminded of that? The death of a child is an unnatural occurrence. It shakes the natural order of life. One should never have to weep over their child's casket.

People no longer know what to say.

In my case, the grief I experienced ten months after Jen's horrible death is not any different from what I experienced ten *days* after her death. The loss is painful, deep, life changing and *present*. I don't expect anyone to understand it. The pain, though, was compounded as my support system began to fade back into the woodwork of their everyday lives. Again, I don't blame them. Why would they want to reach out and be reminded themselves? There have been beacons of support in my family and friends, but far fewer lately. Every now and then (most nights, truth be told) I just wish someone would call and say, "Hey, how are you?" I am pretty sure I'm not hearing that anymore because most are afraid that I'll tell them how I am.

Other times, especially early on, well-meaning friends and family said the wrong thing. I'd be lying if I said I didn't hold it against them. I did, only because I needed to exercise my anger in some way, if only internally. In the weeks when Jen's passing was still fresh, the platitudes pushed my buttons. *No, God didn't need another angel. He could have just made one if He did, right? He didn't need to steal my kid. I call bullshit. No, not everything happens for a reason. Oh, you think it does?. Let's hear the reason. I'm waiting.*

When I sat down to write this book I contemplated, instead, writing a book on what *not* to say when someone loses a child. Months past that phase of the proceedings, I am not sure which is worse; stupid platitudes or the recent weeks of silence. I think silence may be worse. It says a lot more. At least the platitudes were well meaning and I'm secure in the knowledge that I never snapped at anyone over them. The silence now, though? I feel ready to snap again.

I fish a lot these days.

Paddling back down to the bridge, I paused for a moment in the shade of the old metal structure and listened again to the cooing of the pigeons. My ghostly kid-self had gone home for dinner. The images started coming faster and stronger and the tears rolled down my cheeks as I wept anew for my daughter and her future that will never be. It happens every day, but not as often when I'm out on the water. Sometimes it does, though. When I melt down in the middle of what I do to prevent a meltdown, I feel more lost than ever.

I paddled for the launch with no idea what to do next.

Old Home Days

Solitude is the Place of Purification
—Martin Buber

Smack in the middle of the mid-summer fishing doldrums and several uneventful (or *unfishful*) days on the water, Joy and I got messages from a few old friends from high school inviting us to meet at a local bar to watch a popular local band. I'd spent a fair amount of time fishing and an even fairer amount of time in solitude and I was feeling less purified from that solitude than I was distracted, and at times even disheartened *by* it. After losing Jen, distraction was at first a suitable date but, as months wore on, not one in which I was much interested. I certainly wasn't looking for anything long-term. I liked distraction, but it wasn't love and it proved to be as shallow as ever. Spending some time with people we hadn't talked with in decades seemed a good change of pace. It was a different kind of distraction and one that wasn't unwelcome.

In the subtle anonymity of the open-air bar on the harbor, we spotted our old friends before they spotted us. Just a few hundred yards from some of my favorite fishing water, the faces of our friends snapped into focus. If anything, Jen's death had focused my life on the fleeting concept of time. I recognized the faces of our friends, not so different from the passage of time as they were *shaped* by it. I imagine my face to be the same: The same, yet different. It's more different now, I'm sure, bruised with the blunt implements of pain as much as the subtle erosion of time. I don't know if the bruises were as visible as I'd convinced myself they were.

I smiled anyway.

The conversation flowed easily, even for Joy and I who are not the most socially adept people you're likely to meet. There's something about people who knew you when you were five years old that brings a sense of familiarity and comfort when you're just turning fifty. I hoped my old friends felt the same. Of the three women we talked to for a few short hours, there wasn't one there who hadn't become the kind, caring and thoughtful adult five decades into life's journey I imagined they would. If they were disappointed in me, I wasn't by them.

At some point the oldest of our friends, also a writer, asked what I was writing now. I thought hard about it. *The concept of time as a river,* I thought. *The convergence of life and death and what it means to be the parent of a child who is no longer. It's a book about dealing with grief through the distraction of nature* I thought, somewhat glumly.

"It's a fishing book," I offered.

Socially inept, as I said.

She looked at me sideways. "Okay," she said and didn't press it further though I would have allowed it. It's good to have friends who know you, even friends who haven't known you for a long time. The night passed in a meandering current of beer and music, wine and conversation. Lake Ontario reflected the moonlight on the way home. It had been a good night.

The following afternoon, I floated quietly on the turbulent surface of Lake Ontario, a bit farther from shore than I usually attempt when the wind's kicked up. Paddling west into the gusts, I went as far as my arms allowed. The restless wind pushed me back east toward the mouth of the creek. I dropped a clear tube jig to the bottom of the lake and daydreamed as I felt the heavy lead head bounce around and over the rocky bottom fifteen feet below. Every now and then I'd snap the rod tip up as a fish, real or imagined slurped up the bait. Hoping for one of the giant smallmouth bass that aren't at all uncommon along the lakeshore, I flitted between deep contemplation and intense fishing—not an uncommon condition for me these days. I thought briefly again about my old friends the night before and how easily the conversation came after so many decades of silence. It was a warm feeling in a summer of cold comfort. I have an acquaintance fond of saying how they frequently need their "me-time" and I can't tell you how I hate that phrase. I've had all the me-time I'll ever need. I've had one *hell* of a lot of it this summer. I've spent so much time alone I realized it was actually a *treat* to spend some *them-time* with Joy and our old friends instead of remaining selfishly tangled like a fish caught up in the suffocating gill-net of one's own thoughts. You can have my me-time. On second thought, though, no you can't. It's mine. I am, however, willing to share it with you.

When the rod tip suddenly surged downward in a violent arc, I reared up. The equal but opposite reaction didn't so much *tip* the kayak as it put it into a momentary state of potentially dangerous kinetic energy. Nervously locking my feet into the foot pegs, the energy dissipated as the kayak stabilized and I set the hook. Most good smallmouths rocket toward the surface eventually, preferring to duke it out on top of and occasionally above the water. This one stayed deep. It was undoubtedly a good fish. In Lake Ontario, as in most of the Great Lakes, you never know what might be attached to the other end of the line. At the mouth of the creeks, just into the open water, the menu of possible fish is expansive. The fish fought hard, but not vigorously enough to be a muskie or a pike, or even a big channel catfish. It certainly wasn't one of the more rare giant sturgeon, though I wished it was.

One of these days.

Big smallmouth or sheepshead, I thought. It came closer to the kayak, though not without some disagreement. As the big fish eased up through the blue-green murk of the open lake, glimpses of silver in the filtered sunlight told me it was either going to be a silver bass or a sheepshead. Closer now, I could make out the flat, oceanic shape of a sheepshead—a freshwater drum. I wasn't disappointed. Most die-hard bass fishermen can't stand landing a sheepshead. I don't mind. They're fun enough. I guess there's a lot to be said for not being a die-hard bass fisherman, perhaps? Unhooking the gray and silver fish—a good specimen at well over ten pounds—I turned the fish toward the bow of the kayak to pose for a photo. The fish let out a gaseous groan (their other nickname is "croaker") that made me laugh. A sheepshead croak is very much like a human belch. Before I could trigger the camera the big fish gave a final twist in my hands and was out over the side of the kayak and back into the lake, making for the blue-green depths before I even realized what had happened.

Thinking neither of old friends or new, I continued to probe the lake-bottom as the west wind carried me back to the mouth of my creek. Once back, I paddled west again. I don't know how many times I did that. Five? Eight? From an airplane, I must have looked like an old typewriter working to the end of the line before returning with a *ding* to start over again. Other than a small smallmouth (which is not better than a small largemouth or a large smallmouth), no more fish came to the net that day. Still, after two hour of the natural, rhythmic *fish, paddle, return*, I found I hadn't had a single, black, depressing thought for the entire afternoon.

Finally too tired to paddle upwind for yet another drift, I paddled back into the shelter of the creek. Much like the shelter of my old friends the night before, it gave me much needed relief.

It always does.

Days later, when the warmth of summer and the closeness of old friends began to fade into distant memory, a crushing depression returned—though it hadn't ever been far away. Weighing the options between self-medication and self-meditation, I opted for fishing. I hadn't been to the gar creek for a while, and wanted to hit it again before summer faded away completely. I spent several hours on the most secluded section of the river, with only herons and osprey, turtles and gar as my companions. The rhythm of the casts and an occasional small fish kept me occupied enough so my thoughts retained some color other than black. That's a struggle some days. It was peaceful and distracting enough. When I got bored with the fishing, I paddled a little farther as I quizzed myself on the streamside bird species, spending a few extra moments with the confounding warblers and all their varieties. Once I bored with *that* cure for boredom (quite quickly, I must admit), I paddled north, backtracking my last few hours, past the launch and toward Lake Ontario. My gar honey-holes were only a mile away and I paddled steadily toward the more civilized reaches of Oak Orchard Creek. Only a few hundred yards in, I paused in the current. The wind blew gently from the north while the current pushed firmly from the south. The kayak moved in neither direction, but spun quietly in the center of the stream, torn between the pull of the water and the push of the air.

I was quite literally going nowhere and I felt very alone.

Since November 2nd of last year, isolation has been my most constant companion, and is anything but a welcomed friend. I contemplated paddling back to the launch and starting the long drive home. Before I had time to make the choice between fishing forward or paddling back, a small fishing boat puttered slowly past and unexpectedly cut its engine. The older guy in the boat asked if I was gar fishing and I sheepishly told him yes. He said he was bass fishing, but the gar kept hitting his lures and he hadn't seen a bass. To make matters worse, he hadn't landed a single one of the pesky predators that were my current object of affection. Now, it seemed, he *really* wanted to catch one. I explained the rope-fly concept and technique and gave him a couple to try. Sharing intel and tackle among fishermen is commonplace. On Oak Orchard Creek's deep murky pools, there isn't usually anyone to share anything. So as much as I was here to be alone, it was nice to talk to someone—anyone.

Rounding the next bend, I ran smack into a father and two young kids—probably four and six-years-old. A boy and a girl squirmed in the faded orange Coleman canoe, watching their red-and-white bobbers with a white-hot intensity. The father waved me over. Only three minutes past my last encounter with fellow human beings, I was surprised that this pod of people *also* wanted to chat. It was beginning to feel like old home days.

As it turned out, they were running out of nightcrawlers and asked if I might have any he could buy. I didn't, but would gladly have given them my last one, just so he could watch his kids watch their bobbers a while longer. I thought only of Jen, lobbing worm after worm on Harwood Lake, hoping for her next brook trout. At that age, she could never sit still in the canoe, either. We chatted a few moments longer until I suddenly remembered that the little marina where I launch sells worms, and they were ecstatic when I told them. Dad began paddling and I could hear the kids' twittering voices and laughter long after they rounded the bend out of sight.

When I arrived at the gar spot, a pontoon boat was parked there. Mom, Dad and two more kids—teenagers, or pre-teens anyway—sat anchored in the center of the channel in their rental boat. More red-and-white bobbers circled the pontoon boat. I waved and continued on with my fishing, entertaining the kids when I caught a decent gar and held it up for them to see.

"Hey!" Said the younger girl. "Did you see the bald eagle?!"

Her father shushed her and said that I was trying to fish, so don't bother me. I smiled. Watching the family fishing together was anything but a bother.

I had seen the eagle on and off all afternoon, in fact, but I let her point it out to me again. I suddenly didn't feel so alone at all.

Old home days.

The Big Fish Story

I've read a lot of fishing books, almost from the time I *could* read. As far as I can tell it's an official requirement that every fishing book have at least one big fish story. Looking through the rulebook provided by *The Fishing Book Regulatory Committee on Subject Matter Volume XII* last night, I realized I had better include a big fish story in this book. Thankfully, I have a pretty solid big fish story, so the following should keep me from several dollars worth of fines or even losing my literary license. Here goes:

While trying to finish my kayak-fishing book last year, I was still short of several good photos of me with big fish. That's mostly because I don't catch a lot of them. I'm far too content with smaller fish. Rather than risk writing an *expert* book on kayak-fishing that was full of me grinning like an idiot while holding bluegills, small trout and the occasional nice bass, I figured I'd better go out and target some big fish. It was the only way I could appear the expert that I purported to be. Pike and gar are two of my favorite fish, and they both can get pretty big. On the day of "The Big Fish Story," I decided to target northern pike. While pike abound in many of my home waters, I wanted to try a place I haven't fished in many years, but from which I've pulled a lot of pike in the past. Tonawanda Creek is part of the Erie Canal system, and more suburban than I usually prefer to fish, but I knew I'd find pike there.

I'm going to leave out the part of the story in which the power steering in my pickup truck gave out on the way to the creek and how every minute on the stream, I was stressed about getting back home. I wasn't even sure I could get back out of the parking lot, much less navigate the busy Niagara Falls Boulevard that awaited me almost as soon as I left the creek. I'll also leave out the fact it was my truck's last trip anywhere. I sold it shortly after, still sitting in a puddle of its own blood-red fluids. God, that truck pissed me off, but let's not talk about it.

Tonawanda Creek is a busy waterway. Boats far bigger than my little kayak run up and down the creek, some headed out to Lake Erie, while others are just pleasure cruising up and down the canal. The current isn't terrible, but it is substantial when your arms and back are the only source of propulsion. Still, there are several backwaters and islands providing refuge from the current. As I dragged my kayak down the hill from the parking area, across the bike path and arrived at the edge of the creek, I was hopeful.

Immediately paddling for the shelter of a large island, it struck me how hard the current was working to move me in the opposite direction. Once on the lee side of the rock island, I rested for a moment, surprisingly winded. Above me, joggers in brightly colored running clothes passed by at regular intervals, mostly single-minded in their own activities, though some gave a friendly wave. Not many. It wasn't a wilderness experience I was seeking, and it wasn't one I was going to get. My goal was a pike (and hopefully a big one) that would politely pose for some hero-photos with the author before their release. Yep, just that easy.

Pike fishing appeals to me partly because the gear and lures are big, obnoxious and as ornery as the fish. Selecting a minnow lure as large as some of the trout I recently caught, I cast the heavy lure into the flooded timber along the north side of the island and caught the silvery reflection as it pulsed and flashed underwater. *If I were a pike, I'd bite that,* I thought. A moment later a very large largemouth bass smashed the lure. With the heavy pike rod, I brought the bass easily to the side of the boat and held it inside the net while I reached for my camera, secured in front of me on a clamp mounted to the front of the cockpit. Thinking better of it, I knew I had more bass photos than any book publisher would ever care to see. Still, it was a nice fish. *Nah.* I unhooked the largemouth and lowered the net, watching it flick effortlessly back under the log from which it had come.

More bass.

Something from my youth about catching pike and bowfin on a regular basis caused this love affair for the nastier fish that continues to this day. I just think they're cool. Bass are okay. I really like catching bass on the fly rod. They're hard fighters and common enough to be successful with a fair amount of frequency. I think I've landed a lot of big bass over the years simply because I'm always fishing with some outsized lure or crankbait for the predator fish. The bass that are bold enough to hit those offerings are often very big bass. Don't get me wrong, I enjoy every fish I catch, and bass are certainly no exception, but I don't feel the affinity for them that I do for the more notorious species.

It wasn't long before the first pike hit, and then the second. Unlike bass, northern pike aren't afraid to tackle something nearly as big as they are and both of those first two pike weren't much bigger than the lure. The biggest of the pair was maybe eighteen inches and skinny as a snake. I held him up for a moment, his colors glimmering in the morning sunlight. I like pike, even small ones. His malevolent eyes signaled to me that if our roles were reversed, he'd kill me right then and there, no hesitation. How can you not like a fish like that?

Tiring of what appeared to be a nursery for small pike, I paddled around the island. Three large culverts cut beneath the jogging path and beyond was a large backwater I'd often seen from the road but never explored. Picking the largest of the culverts, I ducked and paddled through, though my paddle banged often on the edges and I had to lower all of my rods from their holders to get through the last twenty yards. It was a tight fit and more than a little creepy with all the spiders and webs. Joy would have hated it.

Once through the Mr. Spider's Wild Ride, I emerged on to a small shallow pond. It was an entirely different ecosystem from the deep creek I'd just left, and fish rose all around me. Paddling as close as I dared to the nearest fish, I couldn't quite make out what they were. Quickly piecing together my fly rod, I made only two casts before hooking what looked remarkably like a giant mutant golden shiner. It wasn't though. From my experience back home on Twelve-Mile, I knew this was a Eurasian rudd. *Invasive species*, if you'll recall. In this little pond, they seem to have won the invasion. Pulling down my polarized glasses, I saw that they were everywhere. It was like being plopped down in the world's biggest koi pond. My inner aquatic biologist began thinking what a great food supply the rudd must be to the big pike and occasional muskellunge that inhabit the creek. This area must be a snack bar for the big predators. Quickly paddling around the pond, I noted very few ambush areas that might harbor predators. Braving the Tunnel 'O Spiders once again, I paddled out to the main creek. Where the culvert meets the creek lays a large drop-off to a gloomy blue depth. Still sheltered from the current, if I was a big fish waiting for a dumb rudd to swim out and make dinner of itself, that hole is where I'd be. I paddled over it on the way into the pond, but there was no visible structure and I paid it no attention.

Positioning my kayak just off to the south side of the hole, still within the current break provided by the island, I quickly dropped my large spinnerbait down into the hole. It took a while to hit bottom. I let it rest for a three-count before picking up the slack, and immediately knew I was snagged. I muttered something my mom wouldn't be proud of, and realized the flooded timber from the island must extend down into the blue abyss. I tugged and there was no give. Had to be a tree. I'd have to break off the spinnerbait. *So much for the plan.*

Then the tree shook its head.

I have a lot of big fish stories that start with thinking I'm hopelessly snagged on something on the bottom. This is one of them. If you've caught any big fish, you know that feeling. It's not the vibration of a small fish attacking. It's just a slow side-to-side motion that says *oh, you should not assume you will catch me.* It's menacing. Maniacal. The fish suddenly ran, staying deep and swimming steadily. The kayak spun, following its progress in a half-circle and then starting out into the current of the main creek.

Now this was getting interesting.

A large pontoon boat lumbered down the center of the creek. Thankfully they stopped and looped wide around me because I sure as hell couldn't have avoided them. Still holding my rod for all I was worth, I switched it to one hand, and with the other struggled to paddle backward out of the center traffic lane. I made it back to the relative shelter of the island and suddenly thought the fish was off. Dropping the paddle back into my lap, I cranked on the baitcasting reel. The weight was still there, but it began coming toward me. Wary of some Jedi-fish tricks, I waited for the secondary explosive run. It didn't happen. Still, I've seen some boat side antics best described as *destructive.* As the fish came closer, my tension level rose. *It shouldn't be giving up this easily.*

Once ten feet from the boat, the water clarity allowed me to see what had dragged me better than forty yards. At first I thought *muskie,* but as the fish neared I saw the familiar polka dot yellow markings of a very large northern pike. It was probably the biggest pike I've ever hooked. The giant white spinnerbait looked impossibly small wedged in the corner of those huge, menacing jaws. I waited for the explosion. I prepared myself for mayhem.

It never happened.

I brought the pike up alongside the kayak, certain this was the largest fish of any type I've hooked from a kayak. *There's your picture right there.* I reached for the camera mount. With the camera set to snap a photo every two seconds for as long as I let it, I hit the button and prepared to quickly hoist the beast into kayak for a quick couple of photos, and release her back over the opposite side just as quickly. I had no intention of harming such a magnificent beast for any longer than I had to.

A funny thing happened on the way to that photo, though…I

pushed the big silver button on my waterproof camera and it didn't beep to indicate photography was underway. Spinning the camera around, the text message on the rear screen was plain to see even in the bright morning sunlight: "No Memory Card—Please Insert Card." I had an extra memory card back in my truck that, by then, had probably bled out. But we're not talking about that.

The monster pike finned quietly next to the boat. I think it would have waited there all day. It wasn't only long, but its girth was staggering as well. The northern was a true giant. I wanted to get my hands on it and have that *moment* but, without a camera, there was no sense stressing her by lifting her out of the water. I reached down and grasped the spinnerbait, my fingers perilously close to those massive teeth and jaws. Once freed, she stayed a moment longer as if to taunt me. She then slowly submerged into the depths of the big creek, finally disappearing.

I paddled back to the parking lot and retrieved the spare memory card, but caught only small fish for the rest of the morning. Nothing photo-worthy.

With the completion of this story, I think my Literary License is secured for another year, though my membership in good standing with *Fishing Photographers Piscatorial Society of America* may now be in jeopardy.

It's always something.

Into the Deep Darkness

I often think that the night is more alive and
more richly colored than the day.
—Vincent Van Gogh

A day without sunshine is like, you know, night.
—Steve Martin

Until I was in my early twenties, night fishing was a fairly infrequent affair. I'd occasionally go smelting or bullheading with my best friend Frank and his dad, Tom. Most of the memories, though vague, are of sweltering nights and mosquitoes drawn to the blinding light of Tom's old Coleman lantern. There are other memories of fishing with my brother, dad and my Grandpa Spring on Loon Lake in the Adirondacks that are also hazy from the erosion of time. I remember the four of us sitting quietly in an old rowboat, dropping worms to the bottom of the lake and occasionally pulling out a bullhead, staying until we had a small pail full of them. The remainder of the evening was spent skinning them on a picnic table by the light of the floodlight on the cabin. Good memories, but not very sharp ones anymore.

More recently (if you can call twenty-five years ago more recently, considering that twenty-five years is half of a lifetime for me), I took up night fly-fishing for trout. The first time a call from my old friend Ken

Reed came at 10 p.m. asking if I wanted to go fishing, I was surprised.

"In the morning?"

"Now."

Ken was one of the first *real* adult friends I made as a *real* adult, and he was a good influence on me. One of the basic tenets I picked up from hanging around with Ken was this: If you're invited to go do something — especially fishing—you better have a very good excuse if you don't say yes. This has stuck with me in the intervening years and is one of my basic rules of conduct, as it applies not only to fishing but also to almost anything else. I try to always say yes. If I say no to an outdoor outing, there usually is a good reason and, hopefully, that reason is I'm already doing something else equally as fun.

I met Ken when we were both residents of the famed Catskill Mountains. He was a native. I was a transplant after college. We shared a love of hunting, music and, most importantly at that stage of my life, fly-fishing for trout. We didn't spend a lot of time fishing together, but the days and nights we did were always memorable. Since then we both moved away from the area, but have joined each other in Maine for landlocked salmon fishing as well as here on my home-waters for steelhead fishing. We had some great times together, and I miss his friendship. It's still out there somewhere.

That first night all those years ago, he said we would be fishing the internationally renowned Junction Pool. That is where two of the classic Catskill creeks, the Beaverkill and the Willowemoc, meet in a deep confluence of current. As most die-hard Catskill fishermen will tell you, Junction Pool can often be a gathering place for dozens of tourist fishermen. I'd fished it several times when I first moved to the Catskills. As I learned the area better, there were far better places with far less angling pressure than Junction and the other famous Catskills holes that are all well peppered. You may have noticed in some of the previous pages that I'm not big on crowds. Though fly-fishermen tend to be a cheerful bunch and willing to share information compared to other subdivisions in the angling world, thirty or forty of them together in one place is about twenty-eight or thirty-eight too many for me. I'm not sure I *groaned* when Ken suggested Junction Pool, but he did follow up the invitation with a *trust me.* I may have groaned, I guess.

We arrived at the Beaverkill parking area in pitch darkness, well after midnight. Like me, Ken didn't mess around and was into his chest waders and ready to fish almost as soon as the truck motor had stopped. I liked that about him.

"What do we use?"

"Dry fly, something big."

The Beaverkill and Willowemoc both share a reputation for being *technical water.* It's not that the fish are smarter there than anywhere else, but rather they've been fished so hard they tend to be more finicky than their cousins in lesser known water. Ken's answer was curious. Being an expert fly tier *and* fisherman, I'd expected a *technical* response to my question.

"What are you using, Ken?"

"Adams, size ten, twelve, fourteen, whatever. Anything will work. Cast it out toward the pool and listen for the rises and listen closely for the hit. They'll be hanging over the drop off."

Whatever? Listen?!

We worked down to the edge of Junction Pool, picking our way through the streamside vegetation. Ken pointed me to the Willowemoc side of the pool and said, "Be careful, stay back from the pool. It's *deep*." I knew that, but deep and *dark* are a whole different thing. I watched as he quietly waded over to the Beaverkill side. Ken was only visible in the reflection of the pool because of the lights of a nearby bridge. He used no flashlight to navigate the dark water.

I waded a bit further into the current. Without warning, the sandy gravel under my feet gave way to a depthless, dark abyss. I'd gone a bit too far. Heeding Ken's advice, I backed up from the drop-off. I know from my daylight fishing expeditions that the big pool is impossibly deep for a trout stream, and I had no desire to go swimming. A lost fly rod here would likely be lost forever.

Twenty yards back from the hole, I unhooked my own Adams (big, bushy, *check)* and began false casting. The light from the bridge wasn't bright enough at that distance to allow me to see where I was casting, much less *how* I was casting. I was more well-practiced at fly-fishing back then, but night-fishing required a whole new technique. If my back-cast was too low, I'd only know when it hit the water. If my forward cast and release were off target, I wouldn't know it at all.

Once I'd calmed myself and gotten into the rhythm of this new fishing, I began to hear things clearly. Rising trout were audible *slurps* along with the occasional splashy, tail-smacking rise as well. I seemed to be surrounded by fish, though not a single rise was visible in the pale, distant light of the bridge. I also began *feeling* the tug of the fly line and got better at judging my back casts without the aid of my vision. All my other senses pulled together in order to make up for my sudden blindness. It was truly a new experience.

One rise sounded particularly close and I happened to be in the middle of a back cast. I radically redirected the forward cast, certain that I was about to pierce my earlobe. There was, however, no sudden sting of pain and the line—as far as I could tell—seemed to fly in the direction of the rise. A split-second after I assumed it hit the water, the black surface erupted in what I also assumed was the right spot. I tentatively raised the rod tip and felt the powerful surge of a fish pulling back at me. Racing to the bottom of the six or seven foot pool of water spread before me in the darkness, the trout fought hard. *This is no small, stocked trout.* A moment later, the line began leveling as he raced for the surface. The trout tail-walked twice across the darkened pool. The second time, I momentarily made him out in the distant glare of the bridge lights. When he tired after several moments, I guided him blindly into my small landing net. Wetting my hand, I reached into the net and felt a *very big trout*—well over eighteen inches. I lowered the net to the water so he could breathe, but could not resist digging out my penlight to illuminate what was far and away the biggest Junction Pool trout I'd ever caught in my life. From his acrobatics, I thought the trout might be a rainbow. The small beam of the penlight lit up the brilliant chrome back and blood-red stripe down his side. A Catskill rainbow of that size is a true work of art. In the dimness of the penlight, his colors glowed with a supernatural aura. The fly was out and I released the bow back into the blackness.

Hmm.

More trout came to the net in the darkness. Several small browns, more typical Catskill trout, eagerly grabbed the increasingly frazzled Adams. It doesn't matter. Later on, around two in the morning, another big fish came to the net. This one was a fat brown trout with vivid yellows and browns. In the darkness, I could hear Ken quietly whistle every now and again when he netted a fish. Once I'd grown comfortable with this whole night fishing thing, I found I could look around while I was casting. There's no sense staying face-forward when you can't see a damn thing. I looked to the stars, trying to identify constellations and counting satellites as I continually casted toward the sounds of rising fish. The Milky Way stood out, clearly visible against the dark mountain night, illuminated only by a sliver of moon. The depth of the stars was dizzying and several times I had to return to earth to reestablish my balance.

Ken crept back toward me around three in the morning. We hadn't exchanged a word for the entire evening. While he was still fifty yards away, his own small light illuminating his treacherous path along the darkened rocks, the water exploded next to me, ending with a sharp crack. If it was a fish, it was a great-white shark.

"Holy shit!" I couldn't help myself.

Sitting on the bank and watching me fish, Ken laughed loudly at my outburst.

"Beaver," he said. "Happens all the time."

"Huh."

"How'd you do?"

I told him I didn't know how many I landed—maybe twenty? But that two of them were big.

"You?"

"'Bout the same, but three of them were big."

I nodded.

Somewhat curiously he asked, "*Any bats?*"

I responded that I was sure they were out there.

"No, *I know* they're out there, but sometimes they'll grab the fly in mid-cast. Not pretty when you try to unhook them. Not pretty *at all.*"

I pondered the thought. I'd experienced a few moments where it seemed like something had hit my fly line, but hadn't considered bats. I suppose I should have. Ken sat there a few moments longer, encouraging me to make a few more casts. I thought about bats and how surreal it must be to let your cast go, only to see your fly line rising up in the darkness as if being drawn out into outer space.

Over the next months, we'd make several night trips to various spots on the Willowemoc, the West Branch of the Delaware River, and the Beaverkill, but to this day it's the Junction Pool tickling my memories and imagination due mostly to that first night. It's a place that, in daylight held no interest for me after my first few trips. I haven't fished it—day or night—in twenty years now.

I need to get back.

Harwood Lake

I took Jessica and Jennifer fishing several places when they were little girls, but the first place either of them caught trout was Harwood Lake. A small lake, nestled in the hills of southwestern New York, it's more of a glorified pond than anything else. Once or twice a year, the state stocks a bunch of brook trout and handful of big browns. I'm sure the trout don't survive the summer in the warm, shallow water, but it was always a surefire bet to catch fish. Also, being a put-and-take fishery, even according to the Conservation Department, I never felt guilty keeping a few fish from Harwood for a grilled-trout dinner. Aside from the sketchy trout fishery, Harwood Lake is a fine place to hone your fly-fishing skills. Small, plentiful bass abound along with good-sized bluegills and pumpkinseeds. Large, freak goldfish (presumably released from some local home aquarium) also call the lake home and seem to be doing quite well—for the past thirty years anyway. Always surprising to see in the clear little lake, many of the bright orange fish have grown to a tremendous size and, from the looks of it, they're steadily increasing in numbers. Maybe several generations from now, when the State runs out of money to stock trout in places where they can't flourish, they'll rename it Goldfish Lake. They do seem to be the biggest and most successful "natural fish" in the lake. (Please read my rant on "invasive species" if you haven't already. What do you mean, you haven't already!?).

Sometimes, the family trips to Harwood involved my dad as well. Three generations of us casting away (almost always from the bank) caught trout and bluegill, bass and bullhead. There was always something to keep the kids and their bobbers (and their dad and their grandfather) busy at Harwood Lake. When the kids were a bit older, not quite teenagers, I used to take them out in the canoe to reach the far shore of the lake where the fish were a bit less pressured and a lot less smart. I'd cast the fly around as the girls watched their bobbers, occasionally hooking a nice largemouth on a cork popper or a large, fuzzy Stimulator. I didn't get much fishing in between threading new worms and unhooking the steady supply of kids' fish, but Harwood was always good family time.

More recently, I used Harwood's good graces to get some of the photos for *The Ultimate Guide to Kayak Fishing*. The lake would almost always produce trout on the fly rod and several of the photos appearing in the book were of Harwood Lake trout. One of the beauties of Harwood Lake is that no motors are allowed, reducing the boat traffic to the occasional canoe or kayak and, very often, no other boats at all. I believe mostly due to the fact the fishery simply isn't very good, the lake—even the banks— were quite often empty. It was the perfect stress-free place to take the kids fishing. No houses mark the banks of the small man-made lake, keeping it even more peaceful and quiet. I'm glad my kids got to spend some of their youth there experiencing that quiet.

When Jen and I reconnected after our difficult year of barely speaking, she specifically requested Harwood Lake as one of our first post-war father-daughter destinations. I hadn't fished it in a long time.

"Dad, can I just fish with a worm and bobber," she asked on the phone the night before.

I laughed. Our last outing had been a failed fly-fishing lesson through every fault of my own. I'm a pretty good fly-fishing instructor and have recruited several anglers into that peculiar fold, but I had erroneously tried to teach Jen the basics while seated in the canoe. It was an unnecessarily difficult session and one that had obviously soured

Jennifer on the whole concept of fly-fishing.

Good going, Dad!

"Worms it is!"

The hour-long ride to Harwood was quiet. Often, the quiet time riding to a fishing destination was when I got the most out of Jen. She was not easy to open up, but time in the car usually broke down her defenses a bit. Later on, when she was undergoing chemotherapy and radiation, those rides to Buffalo were a dark shadow of the rides to Twelve-Mile Creek and Harwood Lake. Once at the lake, though, Jen glowed with a big smile as we unloaded the canoe from the truck bed. I could tell that she was up to some mischief.

"What's so funny?"

"Promise you won't judge?"

"I've heard that before. New tattoo?"

She laughed in a bird-like cackle that was pure Jennifer and one that, on my better days, I can still hear if I try hard enough. Hiking up one leg of her shorts, she revealed an enormous lion's head tattoo on her upper left thigh. It was really quite striking and beautiful. I told her that and she seemed relieved. As we loaded the canoe with our fishing gear and rigged up our rods, she went on at length about the tattoo artist, the deal she got, and how excited she was. The lion had always been Jen's spirit animal. A few years later, at her funeral, Jessica wrote a lovely tribute to Jen and *their* private car time, singing selections from *The Lion King* on their way to Jen's treatments. I never heard that until the funeral. In part, what Jessica wrote was that Jennifer held on so long and fought so hard because she didn't want to leave *her pride*. It was true. Jennifer Spring fought like hell and fought through hell to stay with us as long as she could.

I couldn't fathom that anything so horrible lay just ahead on that bright cool morning on Harwood Lake. How could anyone fathom that? If I had been able to see into the future, I may have gone insane.

"That is a great tattoo. Amazing, really."

"Are you just saying that because you're stuck out in the boat with me for the next couple of hours."

This time, I cackled and reassured her that was not the case.

"I'll bet it hurt, though."

"Ohhhh, yeah."

The canoe cut quietly through the water. Jen, twenty years old and full of life, took the bow, eagerly squirming in her seat like she had when she was a little girl. I think she was as pleased at my reaction to the tattoo as she was to be out in the cool mountain air on one more quiet morning in a life full of promise. When we began fishing, she insisted that she thread up her own worm.

"Oh, you really are a grownup," I said, handing her the worm box. Two hours of backyard mosquito hell had resulted in three-dozen fat nightcrawlers. I knew that the few stores between home and Harwood Lake would not be open in the early morning hours. It was worth the mosquito bites so Jen didn't have to be subjected to the horrors of fly-fishing.

"I've gotta learn sometime."

I watched over her shoulder as she threaded the unfortunate worm with care, precision and a healthy helping of *oh, yuck*. Her first trout took the bait almost immediately. Right next to the canoe, she didn't even have to reel but rather swung the brook trout up and over the gunnels, holding it suspended in front of her face to admire the bright coloring of the semi-artificial trout.

"It's beautiful," she said, without touching it.

I remembered the exact instant when she was about eight and hooked her first brook trout on the bank not far from here. Her mouth open in excitement, she was nearly jumping up and down. The mental image is crystal clear because it isn't just a mental image. I captured it on film. Jen with that wide-mouthed grin, flipping the trout up onto the grassy bank while Jessica looked on, her own little-kid fishing rod in her hands. It's one of my favorite photos.

"Dad, can you unhook it," asked the grownup Jennifer, snapping me out of my trance.

"Sure. Swing it back here."

"You probably think I'm a wimp!"

I laughed again. "Not at all. I still can't believe you put your own worm on. This is like a vacation for me!"

"Ha-ha-ha."

I unhooked the pretty little fish and dropped it back into the lake.

"Good going!"

A few moments later, she caught another and another and the cycle repeated itself several times through the morning. I just enjoyed watching her fishing, suddenly understanding some of my older fishing partners just a little bit better in the process. A few more wheels turned in the cogs of the healing process between my youngest daughter and me, and I felt strangely at peace on that little lake with a big history.

"Aren't you going to fish?"

"Okay, okay, but you might need to slow down a little on the *catching* if you want me to start *fishing*."

"Nope, I don't think so. And you have a long way to go to catch up."

I false cast the big Woolly Bugger out toward a patch of lily pads along the wooded east side of the lake and dropped it almost where I had intended. It was promptly snatched up by a very small bass. Pulling him in by the fly line, I released him underwater. A few casts later in the same vicinity a slightly larger bass took the fly, fighting a little bit, and making things at least interesting. Then it was another small bass, which chewed the fly to shreds. In between, Jennifer landed another brook trout.

"Stop!" I teased.

"You're just jealous," she teased back. "All you can catch is *bass*."

I knew I had raised her right.

Having had my fill of nursery-school bass, I directed the next few casts of the embattled fly out into the deeper water where Jen had been catching all of the brook trout. I wasn't surprised when, after a half-dozen casts and slow retrieves, the fly was grabbed by something just as it began to sink below the surface. Raising the fly rod quickly, I felt a heavy pressure that didn't seem quite right for the normally small trout of Harwood Lake. The hole in which Jen had been hooking trout was about ten feet deep, and this one went straight for the bottom. *Bass? Goldfish?* It was big, whatever it was. Applying just a touch of pressure, since I was using a very light tippet, line sizzled out of the reel. That caught Jennifer's attention.

"What is it?"

"I'm not sure. Either a big bass or a big something else."

I hadn't considered it could be a big trout. They're infrequent enough to be called *rare* in Harwood. After giving the fish a little time to tire itself out by carefully playing it from the reel, thanks to the extreme clarity of the little lake I made out the distinct and vivid colors of a large brown trout, though it was six feet below the surface. Jen turned around in her seat to watch.

"Hand me the net, Jen."

"Do you want me to net it?"

"Sure, but if you lose my fish, you did it on purpose."

She slid the small wooden trout net (I don't even know why I brought it, since fish from Harwood rarely require netting) below the surface of the water and I guided the trout into it. Jen hefted the net and said "wow!" It was a beautiful, fat brown trout, with colors like the autumn woods. It probably measured only around seventeen inches, but what it lacked in length it made up for in girth. It was more like one of the lake-run browns I'd expect to see back home than something I could have ever imagined would call this little pond home.

"Photo," Jen said. I held the trout while she fumbled with her phone.

When she was done, I dropped the fish into the net and back into the water next to the canoe where it finned peacefully in its tiny mesh prison. I fumbled for my waterproof camera, temporarily lost in my tackle bag. I found it and handed it to Jen.

"Photo."

She was a wonderful photographer and I cherish the picture she took of that trout and me with my big, stupid grin, not because it was a great fish, but because *she* took the photo. It was a snapshot, a slice of life from *a very good day.* You don't get too many of those—good days or photos of them, that is.

On the way home from our *very good day,* Jen asked again, "You really like the lion?"

"I really like the lion. A lot."

She smiled the sweetest smile and looked out the window. What I wouldn't give to see that smile again.

I made a return to Harwood Lake early this spring in my kayak. Uncle Jud, who we also lost to cancer just a few months ago, stopped in to see us while I was on my return pilgrimage to the little lake in the southern hills. Jud often stopped in to talk fishing and hunting with us.

"Harwood Lake?" Jud said to Joy, knowing very well my attraction to big fish. "Isn't that a little tame for Joel?"

"He has his reasons," she said to her favorite uncle. I'm sure he understood. I *know* he did.

I'm going to try to fish Harwood once more before the snow flies and the kayak is put up for the winter. I don't expect much in the way of fishing, because it *is* a little tame, but I have my reasons.

That Sinking Feeling

Locals call the place The Cow Bridge. Years gone by, The Cow Bridge was a crossing where farmers moved cows from east to west and back across the creek. Back in its day, the muddy, slightly elevated path through the creek provided safe passage for the cows, allowing them an ankle deep crossing between two very deep pools. These days, the only remnants of the bridge are two small points of dry land, reaching a few feet out into the creek on each side. The bridge itself has disappeared, and the two deep pools are now one. And, for Twelve-Mile Creek, an impressive pool it is. I've no doubt that, if the water was clear enough for scuba diving, what lies at the fourteen-foot depth of the pool would make for an interesting documentary.

The Cow Bridge has been something of a personal hellhole. Oh, I've caught fish there—some very nice fish, too. Big bass and pike call the deep pool home both in the cold spring months and in the warmer, less hospitable summer as well. The steady influx of shad and shiners that race through the relatively narrow what's left of the actual Cow Bridge makes it a prime ambush spot for predators. Speaking of predators, two of my biggest bowfin came to the boat from the depths of that big, mysterious pool. In addition to the normal Twelve-Mile denizens, during the spring and fall runs, steelhead and salmon often pause for a rest in the deep pool before continuing on up into the impossibly small upper reaches, such as those in my backyard. Depending on the time of year, almost anything that can be caught in a Great Lake tributary can be caught in The Cow Bridge pool, including channel catfish. *A little slice of piscatorial heaven,* you might think, so *why a hellhole* then, you may ask?

Let me tell you!

The Cow Bridge pool has eaten more of my gear than any single piece of water on the planet. Over the years, I've probably lost the same amount of gear as any other boat-based angler in various places around the Northeast. I couldn't begin to list all the gear I've lost, but it includes cameras, rods, a watch, a couple of hats, and a very nice trout net. Stuff happens and, more frequently, it happens to fishermen. It's an avocational hazard when you spend a large amount of time dangling expensive items over the side of a boat. In a kayak, gear loss takes on a whole new dimension, but almost every angler I know has lost *something* overboard.

The Cow Bridge has been my own personal Bermuda Triangle for gear. I'm sure I lost some stuff there when I was a canoe-fishing kid, but I don't recall any of it. The last few years, particularly when I was fishing hard for research (don't laugh) for *The Ultimate Guide to Kayak Fishing*, I suffered gear loss on an unprecedented scale and it was all at The Cow Bridge pool. On my depth finder, the bottom appears jagged and not at all peaceful. However, it wasn't until I started seriously working that pool with a variety of tactics including cut bait, live bait, jerkbaits, crankbaits, spinnerbaits and just about any other kind of bait you can shake an Ugly Stik at that I realized its gear eating potential. In a few short months I lost several lures, several bait rigs and an anchor. The first time I *almost* lost an anchor, I finally pulled up a sizeable treetop. Lifting a heavy weight while balancing in a kayak (even the stable *fishing* variety kayaks that I have) is a chore on a good day. Add current, the weight of the anchor and a sometimes-disagreeable wind, and there exists the potential for disaster.

My crowning glory of gear loss came on an April fishing trip. Armed with several types of tackle and rods, I hoped to target bowfin with bait.

Any steelhead that might still be stacked in the deep pool would have been a welcomed bonus. Along with that gear was a very nice (read: *not cheap*) baitcasting combo I'd received from Joy as a Christmas present. My plan was to dredge the bottom for bowfin (or catfish, or whatever) with a piece of cut bluegill. I rigged up the smelly bait and reared back to cast the heavy level-wind setup across the pool into the deepest area. Sometime between the backcast and the forward swing, I hooked the not-cheap baitcasting rod with the heavy weight and hook and ripped it from the rod holder over my left shoulder. I didn't realize it until the rod bounced off my head and splashed into the water. In one of those *slooowwww moooootion* moments, I grabbed for the rod as it began to sink out of sight. I missed it by about an inch. One would assume the rod was hooked well enough to remain attached to the bait rig. One would be wrong. I reeled in, praying the line was still attached to the rod. The heavy bait rig, however, was unencumbered by any fishing gear. The rod, as it sank to the full fourteen-foot depth of the godforsaken, gear eating pool, created a strange, feathery signature on the depth finder. It was quite lovely, in fact. It was *extra* fun being able to watch it slowly sink to the bottom. *Just like reality TV!* I spent the rest of my afternoon of fishing, dragging the bottom with a heavy, treble-hook-laden lure, hoping to snag the escaped rod. Of course, *no luck!* What I brought up was branch after branch after log after branch. *No wonder the bottom of that hole eats so much gear*, I thought. At one point, I lost the big lure when it snagged something too large to extricate.

Game over.

I stayed away from The Cow Bridge for a while. Actually, I stayed away from it for the rest of the year. Sometime earlier *this* year, though, I got thinking about that pool and all its possibilities and I decided to give it a go while there might still be a nice mix of big fish available. I carefully selected rods from the rack that were a bit older in vintage and somewhat lacking in pedigree.

Oh no you won't, Cow Bridge!

It was to be the maiden voyage for a smaller, lighter kayak I'd recently purchased on a friend's suggestion. If you don't know much about fishing kayaks, one item you'll see on most of them is an anchor trolley. It's simply a mechanism made of rope and small pullies, with a ring through which you run the anchor line. Depending on wind, current and other variables, the trolley allows you to position the anchor near the bow, stern or side of the kayak to make anchoring in current and wind a bit safer. Well, my friend, it was a *new* kayak. I hadn't yet invested in the anchor trolley. I didn't think it would be much of an issue since the stream's current is fairly light and its mostly steep banks make a good wind break as long as the wind is east or west.

I arrived at the deep pool to find the current stronger than usual from the previous few days' rain. With the creek still not terribly off-color, I thought the fishing was salvageable, but realized as soon as I paddled up to the pool that dropping anchor would be necessary. The characteristically west wind was blowing hard from the north, straight up the creek. I thought long and hard about my own advice against anchoring in current and wind, but decided if I stayed off to one side, in only two or three feet of water, it would be safe enough to anchor, even with the wind and current. I pulled into some emerging lily pads and dropped the anchor into the mud. It settled with a soft plop after which a plume of muddy water rose to the surface.

Perfect.

Casting my traditional white spinnerbait, I caught two nice bass in just a few casts. The largemouths, not in season until June, were a nice surprise for one of the first outings of the year. While not steelhead (or even bowfin), they fought hard, aided by the unusually strong spring current. Happy to boat and release some good fish with so little effort, I was feeling pretty good about myself. Isn't that when things always go bad?

A harsh gust from the north pushed the kayak quickly out over deeper water. The anchor, suddenly dragged off the mud flat, suspended beneath the kayak over the plunging pool. *Dammit.* In my haste to untie the anchor line, it slipped through my cold fingers and plummeted to the depths. Another gust of wind pushed me sideways. I reached quickly to retrieve the anchor before it could snag in the submerged branches below. *Too late.* The sideways sweeping motion of the kayak firmly set the anchor into the branches and debris below. It was apparent after one hard tug-of-war the anchor was going to join my previous anchor as a permanent resident of The Cow Bridge pool.

As I hurriedly rummaged through the toolbox in the small compartment ahead of me, another gust of wind from the north spun the kayak around again. Now with the boat positioned perfectly perpendicular to the current (because I hadn't installed an anchor trolley—against my own damn *expert advice)* the wind blew harder and harder from the north, to my right. The anchor, now firmly affixed to the cleat on the right side of the kayak, pulled the knot so tight that undoing it was out of the question. A million things flashed through my mind as the right side of the kayak leaned into Twelve-Mile Creek and the left side began pointing skyward. Selfishly and perhaps ridiculously, I began thinking how this was going to look: *Local kayak-fishing author drowns in his kayak—didn't follow his own advice!* While I was in no danger of drowning, precisely because I *was* following my Number One Rule and wearing my PFD, I certainly was on the cusp of potentially drowning a lot of gear (including some expensive electronics and cameras). On top of swamping the boat, there was the very real possibility my kayak would fill with water and be tethered to the bottom of The Cow Bridge pool for the better part of eternity, or however long plastic lasts. Only the tree branches, a very nice baitcasting outfit, two anchors, a bunch of lures and some bowfin would be there to keep it company.

The kayak listed into the current and as water bubbled up over the right gunnel, I realized that *stability* is a relative term. It's certainly a stable kayak. I've had it out in waves I wouldn't have dared taken some of the other fishing kayaks and canoes I've owned over the years. Being anchored to the bottom in current and heavy wind, though, tends to redefine any preconceived notions of stability.

The search through my toolbox yielded a pair of side-cutting pliers and I wrapped them around the thin but strong anchor line. With hands that were shaking as much from anxiety as the cold, I couldn't quite make the cutters chew through the line. I made a frayed mess of it, all right, but still it held. Water was now pouring over the right side, soaking my right leg and foot. Behind me, located next to the rod holders in a very inconvenient location was a survival knife given to me by my survivalist-enthusiast brother-in-law, Steve. I never really thought I'd need a real *knife* on the boat but, since it's something I suggested in my book for just such occasions, I thought it would be extremely silly to die because I didn't have one. Twisting around in an unnatural fashion, I managed to snag the bright orange knife without flipping it out into the depths of The Cow Bridge pool. With several shaky yet quick motions, I cut the anchor line cleanly through. The kayak leaned suddenly and violently to the left. So overbalanced was I from the *right hand* tilt, I almost went flying over the left side. I maintained balance, if not composure. If anyone was hiking along the many paths by Twelve-Mile Creek, they were undoubtedly treated to a multitude of colorful phrases I did not learn in Sunday school at the Ransomville United Methodist Church. One of those words was repeated often and with a great deal of enthusiasm.

It was very cathartic.

Once freed from my direct line to the hellhole, the current and wind conspired to send me quickly downstream in small, graceless circles. As I got the kayak under control and pointed in the direction of *my* choice rather than Nature's, I couldn't help laughing. My heart was beating harder than it had in a long time. Though I'd never been in any *real* danger, I had been in *some* danger and once that danger abated, it felt good to be alive. Maybe that's a little melodramatic, since it's only a fouled up anchor story, but it had been a long, *long* time since it felt really good to be alive.

Despite the wind and the current, it wasn't a bad day to fish. The sun shone and fish were rising in another, shallower pool on the way back to the launch. I paddled the kayak up against one of the steep shale banks and stepped out, picking a small flat spot on the bank to stand and cast for a while. It wasn't long before another bass came in. It was just an average bass even for a bass. I unhooked the largemouth underwater and watched him flick away into the murk of my creek. Casting again, I turned my face to the sun. Again, it felt good to be alive. These days, I'll take that anytime I can get it.

A Boat Lies Waiting

I must lose myself in action, lest I wither in despair.
—Alfred Lord Tennyson

I've had several fishing boats over the years, mostly small boats with small motors, canoes and kayaks. When Jennifer and I finally found common water in our post-divorce healing process, it was in canoes and kayaks on a variety of waterways, but mostly on my home creek. Very often when Jennifer had something to ask, something to discuss, or even when she wanted to share her latest ink with her anti-tattoo father, she usually framed it in the form of a kayak-fishing invitation. I never said no. Since then—several years now—the kayak has been my sole go-to for fishing. For practical as well as sentimental reasons, I feel at home and (perhaps more importantly) at peace on a kayak. I'm well suited to quiet paddling on quiet water, and it's well suited to me.

Several months before Jen's death, she talked to me frequently about fishing. As the weather warmed going into the last spring and summer of her life, I promised to take her. The radical brain surgeries and treatments had left her limited, and I worried I was making a promise I could never keep. But then, that happened a lot later on. I did take her out for an afternoon of fishing on the small pier near my home, but she was violently sick after only a few moments. Then there was her final trip on Canandaigua I detailed at the beginning of this book. But even after those ill-fated fishing trips, we talked fishing. We spent enough time talking about medications and treatments, heartache and fate. Our relationship moved from parent and child to patient and caretaker. When we talked fishing or photography, though, we were just Jennifer and her dad.

I'd always wanted a square stern canoe and, when it became painfully apparent that she'd never kayak with me again, I looked around the area for one. Securing a beautiful, vintage aluminum Michi-Craft after a few days searching, we quickly purchased a small outboard motor for it. By late August, it was ready to go. Stable enough to safely take Jen, even with her balance issues, I figured that lovely old canoe on our home water would be the last place my daughter and I would ever fish together. I hurried to get everything ready, knowing that time was running short.

Only a few short days after the boat and motor were registered and ready to go, Jennifer suffered the first of two major seizures. The seizure resulted in a hospital stay and decreased function. Her memory and cognitive ability had already been eroded from the advance of the brain cancer, but the seizure set her back in other ways. She lost most of her strength and most of the use of her left side. Not giving up, she underwent sometimes-painful physical therapy and fought to regain the use of her left side. She never would. It was the beginning of a quick downward spiral from which she'd never return.

God forgive me, I needed a break from the heartache of my afternoon-shift with Jen one day. At a breaking point (in a long line of breaking points), I decided to take Joy out in the new canoe to fish for a few hours. It pained me to take the boat on its maiden voyage without Jen, but it was good to get on the water for the first time in weeks. Using not the new outboard motor, but a small electric motor, I took Joy to the lower reaches of Oak Orchard Creek. We cast for gar, though we didn't land any. I'd wanted to show Joy the great pods of gar and we found them easily. *Strange creatures* she called them as they slapped at our rope flies and followed the lures to the side of the boat. I agreed wholeheartedly.

The electric motor lost power on the way down the creek. Though I'd find out later it was just a loose connector and could easily be remedied, I hadn't been able to diagnose it on the water. We had to paddle back, against the current. It wasn't insurmountable, but never was that canoe designed for paddling.

This past spring, long after Jen had passed, we decided to try Silver Lake for some early season pike in the boat Jennifer never got to ride. The brand new, shiny motor started hard. I blamed it on the cold. It had run fine in the test tank at home, but something didn't seem right. Soon though, after nearly tearing my arm off trying to get it running, we were purring down the lake to the north end where I'd caught pike in the kayak a week earlier. Once at the opposite end of the lake from our launch point, the motor died. For a few minutes, I pulled and pulled and pulled and finally ran out of energy. We decided to fish for a while and let it cool off. We didn't get any pike, and the wind started buffeting us. I pulled the cover off the motor and checked the plug, the gas filter. I checked *everything*. It looked fine, yet after pulling and pulling and pulling and pulling, nothing happened.

Knowing it would be a tough paddle back up the lake, into the wind, Joy and I both muttered about our last trip when the *other* motor conked out. I'd never had such bad luck with a boat and wished more than once we had just taken the kayaks. Stopping halfway up the lake for another round of attempted motor starting, we were again stymied by the reluctant motor. It took a full hour of hard paddling to get back to the launch. We didn't dare stop, because the wind had become so fierce that to do so would have meant dozens of yards of lost ground for each break we took. By the time we reached the relative safety of the cove where the state launch was located, we were exhausted.

As we loaded the boat from its second unsuccessful trip I thought about my broken promise to Jennifer. I told her I'd get her out there just as soon as she was able. The last time she asked me, she was only a few weeks from that dreadful November 2nd.

"Dad, do you really think we'll get to get out in the new canoe together?"

Not for the first time, I lied to my dying daughter. "Of course."

I think we both knew it was a lie and it seems somehow fitting that her boat wouldn't work.

I could write a book of the things that we talked about to pass the hours during Jen's battle, but I don't know if I'd be able to hold it together long enough to type them all out. I could write Volume Two on the things Jennifer said that broke my heart, but I don't know if *you* could get through reading it. I'll share this one with you though:

Shortly after the conversation about fishing together again before cold weather, I was helping Jennifer get out of bed. She was unable to do it safely on her own anymore, and we all took turns helping to hoist her up and into her wheelchair or to the bathroom. Jen and I always joked about it being the *father-daughter dance*. The sense of humor my kid exhibited during those dark, painful days has forever made her a hero in my heart. One day, as we'd done dozens of times, I helped her sit up and she wrapped her arms around my neck so I could help her get to her wheelchair. No words were exchanged. No jokes.

Jen began to sob.

Her voice now hushed to a whisper from the ravages of the cancer and its treatments, she said directly into my ear, "We're never going to have a real father-daughter dance."

"Don't say that, kiddo."

"You've gotta accept it, Dad. We're not going fishing again, either."

"Stop, Jen, please."

I lowered her back onto the bed and we sobbed together. It wasn't the first time, though it was one of the last.

As I write this chapter, Jen's been gone ten months. I can still hear her voice saying those words. I've been wracked with nightmares a few times a week for ten straight months now. Nightmares aren't the hardest things

I deal with. Eventually I wake up. Even in my waking hours, I hear that breathy, labored voice trying to say goodbye, trying to tell her dad to be strong just a few weeks before leaving us forever. If time is a sort of a river of passing events, I'm on a constant loop of those bad days and bad memories coming back around and around again. The current hasn't carried those away though some days it seems as if it's taken everything else. I'm sure clinically it's PTSD combined with grief and depression. Either way, I haven't gotten a break from it. Not for one day. Sometimes, I can get a few hours of peace, then only if I have sufficient distraction. This is why I have spent more days fishing these past months than I have in my entire life. It's my only escape. It's the only one that works, anyway. *Fish, fish, fish, fish, fish.*

Most days, even a bass will suffice.

The shiny canoe I bought for Jen still hangs in the rack in the garage, along with the kayaks. It's an aluminum memorial to what might have been, as if I needed yet another. I haven't gotten around to selling it yet, but I probably will. Every now and then I knock on its metal hull, just to hear it clang. Mostly what I hear is Jen asking if we'll ever get out in it.

"Do you really think so, Dad?"

At least I can still hear her voice.

Tuesdays, Fridays & How I Do It

The question I get asked most often is *how do you do it?* Meaning, to a lot of my casual fishing friends and non-fishing friends, it seems like I have a lot of free time. *Free time,* of course, is all relative. The truth is, most die-hard people I know in any field *find* a way to do it. Whether hunters or fishermen, photographers or amateur artists, people with a passion find a way to *do it.* I hear frequently that I must have a really good job. It is a really good job, and I try to do a good job at that too. I've worked at it long enough that my hours are now more flexible than they used to be. That said, flexibility was not always the case. I used to work a variety of swing shifts that were inflexible as hell. When my kids were young and I was in my twenties and early thirties, I used to work fifty or sixty hours a week. Still, though, I managed to feed whatever current obsession had me under its spell. For a long while, it was fly-fishing for steelhead. Later on, when dogs and pheasants dominated my dreams and daydreams, I found time for them as well. Now that I've come full circle back to fishing at the ripe old age of fifty, I find time for my kayak fishing pursuits. On top of all those endeavors, I carve out time to write about them.

How do you find the time? I hear that a lot.

This isn't a how-to book and was never meant to be. I don't like how-to books, except the one I wrote. (*The Ultimate Guide to Kayak*

115

Fishing—available at fine booksellers everywhere!). I am not a preacher, but rather a lowly gar fisherman. I've no desire to sell you my testament to a life well lived. Sales are not my thing. Rather than tell *you* how *to,* I'll tell you how *I* do it.

1. *Just do it.* I know, you think you know me, and possibly you think that I'm flippant. I've heard that word my whole life, mostly pointed in my direction by well-meaning people who don't know how to have fun. You may know me by now and I am *sometimes* flippant, but I stick to this one and that's why it's number one. If you're passionate enough to want to do something, you don't need me to tell you *just do it.* The truth is, if it's something you believe in and brings you satisfaction you will, by default, *just do it.* So my advice is to run with that and *just do it.* If it's not enough of a temptation to *just do it,* it's probably not something you'd do much anyway, even if you won Powerball and had all the time in the world. I'll give you this one little modifier: If you *love it,* just do it. You don't have another choice and if you think you do, that other choice is likely to make you miserable. Follow your dreams, even your unimportant daydreams and just do it.

2. If you can't *just do it,* make it happen so you can. A recent visit to my doctor resulted in discussing a conversation he had with another patient. That patient, suffering from high blood-pressure and anxiety, said his job was killing him. He wanted the doctor to tell him what to do. The doctor, whose judgment I trust, said simply *find another job. Make it happen.* Do I mean you should quit your job to find more fishing time? No, not necessarily. What I mean is that you shouldn't be miserable. Jen's short life taught me many things, chief among them was that work isn't everything and that quality of life *is* everything. It's gone too soon. Make it work.

3. Sacrifice. Do I mean you should sacrifice your health, your wealth, your family life or anything else of value for a little fishing time? Of course not. What you *may* sacrifice though is a little time on the couch, a little time in front of the television or a little dent in your Netflix binge-watching time. When I get home from work, I'm often tired. Fifty-years

old seems to be a benchmark in energy decline. I felt one of those declines at thirty-five (though, in retrospect it seems laughably minor), and a far greater one this past year as I passed the half-century mark. These days, I have to convince myself to get out there, strange though that may sound when it comes to something I'm so passionate about. When I get home from work feeling fat, tired and lazy, there's nothing more I'd like to do than turn on the news, grab a beer and succumb to the overwhelming gravitational pull of the couch. The point is though, if I am willing to sacrifice the siren song of the couch and a few hours of leisure, I'll find myself out on the water. *And,* once out on the water, my energy level returns to what it was after several cups of coffee in the early morning, and I can't believe I ever contemplated not going. All I've sacrificed is a few hours of doing nothing in return for a few hours of doing something I enjoy. I won't say this is easy, especially if you have a physically or mentally demanding job, but it can be overcome. In the end, when practiced correctly, you're sacrificing a few hours of pointless nothingness for a few hours of pointless enjoyment in the company of nature. I'd rather have pointless enjoyment. In fact, the very definition of fishing (unless you make your living at it) is pointless enjoyment. If that's not the real definition, it should be.

These three rules on which I've loosely based my life seldom fail me. I think most people have a lot more free time than they care to admit. I know several rabid sports fans for whom hours and hours spent in front of the television, placing their hopes and dreams on a bunch of millionaire spoiled brats is the greatest entertainment. I know that many outdoorsmen are avid sports fans. That includes several good friends. Sorry if this makes you bristle, but I don't get it. Maybe it's because I live near Buffalo and investing your dreams in those teams is a fool's errand. I don't know. What I do know is that if I get a fishing invitation on a Sunday afternoon during a Bills game, I'm going fishing. Or hunting. Or taking the camera out. I'm doing something. *Me.* I'm not sitting on the couch, getting fatter and wasting my energy on things over which I have no control. Do I have any control over whether the fish will bite? No, not really. But if I fumble a fish, it matters more than if a running back fumbles a ball, at least to me.

I fish a lot on Tuesdays and Fridays. Monday, the work stress and catching up on emails and things that came up over the weekend eat up my day. Tuesdays, once things are a little more under control, usually work for some time on the water. The rest of the week is usually when Monday's plans come to fruition and I keep my nose to the grindstone. If all has gone well, I find Friday afternoons to be my next best bet for fishing. If I looked through all of my fishing notes for the past year, I'd bet kayak-money that most of them were Tuesdays and Fridays. While Tuesday is a tentative step into my *real life* outside of work, Friday is the glass of champagne celebrating the end of the week and the beginning of a weekend full of possibilities.

I can't tell you what to do. If I *could* tell you what to do, I'm not sure you'd be any happier. All I can say once again is life is short. I always knew that, but a really great twenty-three year old woman with no time left brought that home to me last year. If you have that free hour, go do something you love. If you have a free weekend, go somewhere you've thought about going. If you have only an hour, use it. Use it well and use it up. Use the hell out of it. Use it like you'll never see it again. Don't ask me how I do it. It's not always easy, but I do it and you should, too. Not tomorrow. Not next week. They might never get here. Wet a line, go for a walk in the woods. Don't wait.

Breathe in the things that help you breathe. That's how I do it.

Bits of Red Brick

Four-Mile Creek, another small tributary emptying into a quiet estuary before continuing on to make its contribution to Lake Ontario, is very much like Twelve-Mile Creek, only smaller. Long gravel runs pass beneath mature maples and oaks, making for lovely scenery during the fall salmon runs. At some point in its history, though, the stream got hemmed in for several hundred yards by a golf course. Warm weather fishing in that stretch always means being watched by a golfer or two on one of the small bridges spanning the stream. Most strike up a conversation, some don't. The two distinct sports intersecting at the water can create interesting interactions. Although most of the golfers are polite, I've ducked more than once as a ball flew overhead without the customary warning *"fore!"*. I'm not sure they go home and say "most of the fishermen were polite," but I hope so. Either way, I've never hit anyone with a back cast, and neither do I bear any golf ball scars.

Along with band and fly-fishing, photography was another of my nerd credentials as a kid. In an era before everyone snapped trophy-fish photos on their smart phone I documented my fishing expeditions on this tiny trout stream only two miles from my house. Thirty-five years later, I'm still trying to figure out how to photograph myself with a steelhead and release it with both of us still in good health. During this lifelong learning process, I've never killed a fish though I have drowned a couple of cameras.

I still have the pictures from back then. Somewhere they lie in darkness among the boxes, waiting to be unpacked. In reality, there's no need to find them. It takes no effort to visualize the faded prints—silver fish on the bank next to my cheap fly rod, bits of brick from an unknown source flecking the gray gravel of the stream bed, artistic highlights to the trout's red stripes. The prints, seldom well composed and often just a blurred, abstract impression of a trout making its final flop back into the stream, were prized possessions of my youth. I still cherish those discolored old photos, tangible links to memories that haven't quite faded.

This year, late March came and went without a fish on Four-Mile. I'd done better in the ditch back home. As I'd promised my new fly rod, I stopped to check the small stream often. April saw angry flood waters quickly recede to near-drought emptiness in the tributary. Then the flood began. Stream conditions were volatile, swinging wildly from feast to famine to flood. By then I'd begun carrying my waders and rod with me to work, certain on any day I'd stop at the bridge and see a pod of the bright silver fish splashing about in one of the roadside runs—an excellent predictor of what the action in the rest of the stream might be. It didn't happen and I eventually turned my angling attention elsewhere. As the trees began to bud and leaf out, I knew I'd once again missed my chance on my favorite small creek. How long had it been since I'd caught a fish there? At least several years, I thought. One quiet evening, I paged back through some more recent photo albums. Nothing. Farther back on the shelf I went deeper in time until I saw the smiling faces of my friends from Maine, posing with an impossibly large fish on the bank of the impossibly small stream. *1999. Can that be right,* I wondered? Can it be eighteen years since? I slowly sifted through the photos, noting the red brick flecks interspersed with the gravel and stones over which the stream spilled. Placing the album back on the shelf, I sighed as I quickly organized the rest of the photo books. They ended at 2004, the last year I used film. Despite my love of digital photos, there's something comfortable and concrete about those old books of images. I return often to those plastic pages—the original hard drives. While the photos on my computer don't ever fade, those gradually disappearing prints are a poignant reminder of time moving on. As if I need one.

After a period of early May rain, I paused by the stream. I don't know why. Once the maple trees stretching over the gravel runs begin to shade the water with their red buds, the run is over—and the buds had already begun turning into leaves. I suppose what made me stop was just the glowingly optimistic soul of the avid fisherman.

I know, that made me laugh too.

A half-dozen steelhead with no right to be there chased and raced around the bridge pool. I'd since stopped carrying my fly rod, of course. *Of course!* I watched the pod cruising up and down the stream, splashing and fighting and doing what lake-run trout do when they're confined to a few inches of water. I was mesmerized. Memories of youth and of 1999 came back with each loud splash echoing up under the highway bridge.

Returning a half-hour later, I fished hard. Perhaps *too* hard. It takes countless casts to catch one of the big fish, but it only takes a few too many to shut them down and scare them off. The presence of those huge trout at my feet made my heart pound and I fished hard and I fished far too aggressively. Several fish left the first wooded pool, heading south into the golf course. I reeled in and waited. Ankle deep in the cool water, I attempted my best blue heron. Five minutes later four fish moved up the stream, hovering on the gravel in front of me. I resolved to count to one hundred. Resolve is a funny thing and I made it to forty before letting the white Woolly Bugger drop upstream of the closest pair. The line hesitated. I raised the rod tip and a small male steelhead leapt from the water, pulling line as he raced about the small pool. The water came alive with unseen trout, spooked from their hides by his animated thrashing. He didn't come easily to the net, expressing some intellectual concern over the ease with which he let himself get fooled. So ecstatic was I to land a steelhead in the small wooded pool for the first time in almost two decades, I didn't even take a photo. That doesn't happen often.

The fish kept coming all afternoon and into the evening. Naturally, I took the next day off work. It's what you do when the run suddenly hits. As I suspected, the next morning the stream was swarming with trout. The run that "never was" became one of the best twenty-four hours of small-stream steelhead fishing in my entire life. Some nosy fisherman must have reported my car parked near the bridge to his friend and so on. By mid-morning, I was no longer alone. A half-dozen fishermen, alerted to the strange, late-run goodness, made their way down the muddy slope from the road, planting themselves at various intervals along the stream. All were friendly. The ones who arrived in pairs chattered excitedly about the fish. I talked to them for a bit, imparting my meager intel while giving away a Woolly Bugger to a desperate looking kid. I wished them all luck before departing for a quieter hole.

I'd avoided the golf course up until this point. Hoping for a bit more solitude, though, I walked the grassy banks, ducking under the first golf cart bridge. The water between that bridge and the next boiled with fish. It was not normally a place I'd fish but I dropped my camera pack and got immediately to work. A small audience of two golfers sat on the bridge, watching carefully as I fought one tenacious, hook-jawed male. A very small round of applause and laughter greeted me as I unhooked and released the fish, getting a face full of tail slime in the process. It wasn't precisely what I'd describe as *solitude*, but the non-fishing observers were not unwelcome. I fished the golf course run for two more hours and couldn't tell you how many fish I hooked, each prettier than the next. I *can* say with certainty that if it were 1999, I'd have run out of film.

Departing the greens or fairways, or whatever golfers call them, I continued up into the woods. Several pools and runs snake among the mature oaks and I found fish there as well. I don't ever recall seeing such a concentration of trout in this very small stream. The Woolly Bugger responsible for the last four fish was a tattered remnant, not at all representative of the fly it had once been. More fish came to that fly until I finally retired it; now little more than a wisp of white and a bare hook. I explored further upstream than I'd ever been, even as an adventurous teenager. Eventually the water was too small for the big trout, but I continued on, hoping maybe to find the ruins of the old mill or farmhouse supplying the creek bottom with its red accents for the last thirty-five years, despite the interceding decades of scouring floodwaters. I never did find it.

In two short days, the mysterious run would end as abruptly as it started. One day the trout were just gone. The new Nikon lens, purchased only a few weeks earlier, bore a one-inch scratch from an enthusiastic thirty-two inch female steelhead that decided I wasn't releasing her quickly enough. I have the photos: big, colorful fish; clear water; bits of red brick scattered among the smooth, polished gravel; the creek shaded by maples and oaks with occasional glimpses of the golf course just beyond. During the warm summer, I've often flipped open the laptop to look over those photos to relive the phantom run of fish on the tiny tributary. The colors stand out as clearly as the day they were taken. Someday I'll print them and place them all into a photo album where they can properly fade.

The Photo Shoot

No man really knows about other human beings. The best he can do
is to suppose that they are like himself.
— *John Steinbeck*

I've always considered myself a fisherman first and a supermodel second. Because of that, the woman barking orders at everyone near the boat launch was beginning to get under my skin. Two-dozen people milled around the launch, unloading their kayaks while waiting for the coordinator of the event to arrive. Several kayaks were touring models with a handful of fishing kayaks mixed in, like mine. In the meantime, the cranky wannabe coordinator continued barking about this and that. She had decided that we should all wait at the launch for the coordinator to arrive and she was starting to aggravate me. One of my kayak-fishing friends I'd drafted into this endeavor was also showing signs of wear.

"These people are weird," Randy said, surveying the kayak gang. He'd had a bit longer to observe them.

"At least there are a couple of kayak fishermen," I offered.

They had nice boats. *Much nicer than mine,* I thought. I didn't have kayak envy, though. That wasn't the problem. I just hoped they weren't good fishermen. I guess it was more prayer than hope. *The Insecure Angler,* anyone?

Looking out over the large Lake Ontario bay, my itchy fishing finger took over. Dragging my big green kayak down to the water, I waded in and hopped into the seat. I wasn't surprised when Randy showed up right behind me.

"Don't you think we should wait for Bill?!" Asked the woman who assumed she was temporarily in charge.

"No."

I was polite, but she didn't seem pleased that I didn't offer an explanation. As soon as I was on the water, my blood pressure dropped significantly as the woman contented herself with ordering younger and less opinionated kayak enthusiasts around by the launch. Randy and I paddled our separate ways, both staying within sight of the group so we'd know when the festivities began.

I'd recently written *The Ultimate Guide to Kayak Fishing* and in the course of promoting the book became friends with a local outdoor writer and TV (I'll tell you about the TV appearance some other time) host who also happened to be the local outdoors promotions guy. He was involved with putting together next year's Niagara County Outdoors promotional materials, including pamphlets, websites, and the like. This year they'd decided to focus, in part, on the kayaking opportunities in our area. With all of the help Bill had given me in promoting my books over the past couple of years, I couldn't say no when he asked me to be part of the photo shoot. Besides, it sounded rather fun. I suggested that Randy come along, as well. I'm not sure he thanked me later, but he's a very good fisherman and much more photogenic than I am. If I failed to land a fish for the photographer, I figured Randy could probably pull it off.

In my brief conversation with Bill over plans for the day, it seemed as if he just wanted us to do a little fishing and call the photography boat over if we landed a fish or two to do a close-up. I pictured Bill and a photographer hanging out with the pod of kayakers, snapping a few photos in the morning sun while Randy and I did our thing. I certainly wasn't averse to taking the morning off of work to do some fishing, even if a photographer accompanied us.

Of course, it wasn't quite that simple.

I realized when the photographer showed up at the dock with three assistants and cases and cases of photo gear this wasn't going to just be your basic grip-and-grin fishing shoot. Not even close.

Of the three-dozen or so people who ended up a part of the photo-shoot, the first one singled out for special attention was…me. The photographer and his assistants couldn't have been nicer, but this was not to be a *do your own thing and we'll shoot a few photos* affair. Oh, no, my friends! With Bill piloting the big fishing-turned-photography boat, the photographer carefully positioned me for maximum lighting. Not just *turn this way* and *turn that way*. It was a matter of *just another inch or two*, and back an inch or two. All right, maybe it wasn't *inches*. Mind you, this was all done in two boats, one of which (mine!) had no power other than my paddle and there was a stiff breeze ushering in the sunrise. The commands to position, fish, reposition, fish, reposition, turn your face to the left, turn your face one-centimeter to the right, seemed endless. Not that it wasn't fun (and interesting to watch the photographer work), but it sure as hell wasn't fishing. When he began to ask me to cast (to a specific spot, while perfectly positioned, while maintaining a serious look—which I can't pull off on a good day) on a three-count, things became even more challenging. Hanging off the side of the boat, he leaned perilously out over the lake while an assistant (whose demeanor may or may not have indicated she was his spouse) held onto his belt. It was a spectacle and, considering that he seemed at any moment to be about to go overboard with ten or twelve thousand dollars worth of camera gear, I found it hard not to watch.

"Don't look at me!" He said, amicably enough. "You're fishing."

I am?! Still it was fun, as a new experience anyway.

Shortly afterward the photographer took on a new affect, talking as if he were a Hollywood director shooting a feature film.

"Now, Joel…let's see. This time I think you look like you're just happy to be here. Look at the sky!"

It wasn't difficult to muster a smile, since I was laughing on the inside. "Joel...you're doing great. I think you're serious now."

If you only knew...

"You're going to paddle toward the camera boat. Maybe your face is determined this time."

I'm pretty sure my face was still stuck in an immature grin. I'll let you know when the brochure comes out.

It wasn't long before they moved on to Randy. Younger, better looking, and with nicer gear than my own, he would have been my *first* choice. I began getting the sinking feeling (a little kayak humor) that Bill may have put them up to photographing me first. They spent well over 20 minutes with me, and probably a half-hour or more with Randy. Paddling up to the boat to talk to Bill while Randy had his 15 minutes times two of fame, Bill said, "Well the camera seems to like Randy!"

"Ageism!" I said.

One of the young assistants turned around to assure me that I did fine. But after noting to him that it was nothing of the sort, I added, "Joking...I was joking."

"Oh," he said, obviously not used to hanging out with fishermen.

Once Randy's shoot was over, they gathered together the pleasure kayakers and asked them to perform some stunts like "paddle over there" and "paddle back this way." They didn't have to work nearly as hard as Randy or me. I noticed the two other kayak fishermen hanging back out of the photo area, and felt a bit bad that all the kayak-fishing attention had been focused on us. I wouldn't feel too bad for very long. Bill told us to get out there and do some fishing and to call his cell-phone as soon as one of us landed a fish. He said he'd like a bass, then a pike preferably. We laughed, assuming he wasn't serious. He might have been. Randy is a tournament fisherman, and a very good one. I hoped my propensity for unintentionally landing big bass would hold out. I figured (and so had Bill) that between the two of us we had a better than average chance at getting bass. If we got too far removed from the photo-entourage, we decided we'd just hold the bass underwater in the net until we could rendezvous with them. Comfortably away from the large group, I began fishing hard. I wasn't paying attention to Randy, but assumed he was working the water pretty thoroughly, as well.

While it may have been a banner day for photography light, it was anything but a good day for fishing. I cast and cast, switching lures and rods and tactics. In the course of an hour or more, I didn't hook a single fish. I did have one solid hit that may or may not have been a bass or a rock.

Well into the second hour of fishing, I hooked a largemouth bass. It flipped around the side of the kayak, putting up an admirable fight before giving up. Guiding the bass into the large rubber landing net, I dug the cellphone out of my dry-box and called Bill. They were farther up one of the bay's feeder creeks, a fair distance from us. I asked Bill if they wanted to meet us, but he said they were well into the group paddling shots up the creek. He asked if I could paddle up and meet them. Kayak fishing often calls for on the spot contortions, such as when a four-foot fish is thrashing on the very small deck of a ten-foot kayak. Almost everything is done with a paddle in your lap, to begin with. Of all the antics I've been forced to perform in a kayak, paddling (a two-handed operation) while holding a short-handled landing net containing a fish that must stay submerged is not one of them. It took me a minute to figure out how to pin the net under my left knee, while keeping it perfectly submerged, but not *so* submerged that the bass might swim out. The heavy drag from the net made paddling a chore, but I figured it out by the time I reached the larger group. They paused the group kayak photos, informing them they had to stop for a few minutes to get a photo of my bass and me. I figured a few quick snaps, release the fish, and we'd be on our way.

I can't remember being wrong so many times in one day.

Asking me to wedge my kayak back into a small channel in the cattails, the photographer went back into Hollywood Mode. He had me lift the fish out of the net countless times, turning it this way and that. "Look at the fish, not at him. Use your right hand, reach over with your left hand. Turn the dorsal fin toward you. Turn its belly toward you."

I don't know how many minutes this went on, with a fleet of kayaks hovering impatiently behind the camera boat, including Randy who seemed to wear a bit of a grin at this spectacle. Every thirty seconds or so, the photographer would say, "Okay, let him breathe for a minute." And then he'd have me haul the fish back out for seemingly (or *actually*) a hundred more high-speed shots. Each time he said, *let him breathe,* I thought *okay, when do I get to breathe!?*

Finally he said, "Okay, I think we're done." I placed the fish back in the net for a moment and noticed one of the photo-assistants whispering in the photographer's ear.

Oh no.

"Joel, I think we'd like to try a slightly different angle."

I told him that would be fine, though I thought before too long I might be holding up a dead fish. He wasn't okay with that, thankfully. I didn't think he would be, though the bass was none the worse for wear, other than being returned to the water a little bit farther from home than he likely ever traveled.

I watched, fascinated, as the photographer's people brought out a very expensive looking aerial drone. Asking the pleasure paddlers to form up in single file, he shot them from high above. I'm sure the line of kayaks in the small feeder creek made for an impressive photo, and I look forward to seeing it. The photographer was very creative, not only in our faux fishing photos, but also in working with the rest of the group. No matter the occupation, it's always impressive to watch a pro at work. Being a photographer myself, I felt a twinge of jealousy looking at the gear he so reckless dangled over the side of a boat.

While we are on the topic of jealousy, one of the two other kayak fishermen paddled up to me after the bass-shoot and asked what lure the bass took. I gladly told him. He didn't, however, seem interested in fishing. While we sat hull-to-hull, I admired the high-end fishing kayak. In fact everything *in* the fishing kayak was high end. Even his clothes were high-end. I dressed for the occasion, and still felt like a bum compared to him. *At least I caught a fish.* After a moment of silence, I asked if he'd like one of the spinnerbaits I used. I give away a lot of stuff on the water.

"No, I really don't want to fish here."

I looked around at the pleasant little cattail-lined creek and the open harbor beyond and wondered why. I was a bit bewildered. A very small alarm bell went off in my head and I wondered if this was one of those high-end kayak-fishing guys who had enough money for the most expensive gear and absolutely no clue about fishing. I've seen a few of them—and not just in the kayak-fishing world.

I couldn't resist, and asked him why he didn't want to fish. Randy paddled up quietly next to me, perhaps curious as to the answer.

"I don't want to damage my gear."

Damage…wait…what? There couldn't me a more innocuous place to fish with less risk to damaging gear than this. Randy shot me a quizzical look that mirrored my thoughts.

Perhaps sensing my alarm bells going off, the other (non?) fisherman asked, "Do you do salt?"

Again, my cynical mind got buffeted in a wind of confusion. *Salty crackers? What?*

"Saltwater, I mean. Do you fish in saltwater? I'm going to fish Chesapeake Bay next week."

Living four hundred miles from the ocean, I had to admit that would be a rarity on my limited travel budget.

He paddled off, at least wishing us well.

"He's afraid of damaging his gear here in the creek, yet he's going to fish in the ocean? Does he know about sharks? Shipwrecks? Coral reefs? Whales?! "

I was stretching it a bit, having no oceanic fishing experience.

"I told you they were weird," Randy offered.

We never caught another fish unless you count the hotdog-sized pike that Randy landed during my extended bass-shoot. He didn't count it so I'm not going to either. It was an interesting day, certainly unlike any other fishing day I've ever experienced.

That's worth something.

Loon Lake

No sound embodies the spirit of wilderness like the midnight cry of a loon over still water. The message is lonely, yet strangely hopeful. They fill the otherwise empty night, saying simply, "Hey, I'm over here." Their mournful wailing seldom goes unanswered. The call of the loons at Loon Lake has punctuated almost every summer I've ever known, from my youngest years through this past summer. The sound has woven a thread through my entire life, through its most youthful days of fishing, to the dark days of the last two years and now the aftermath. Every year I watch the calendar I keep in my office, waiting for that week in July. I never write "vacation" on the schedule. Instead it's simply "Loon Lake". This year, Loon Lake can't come soon enough. I look forward to lying in bed under the open window, waiting for the call of the loons, as much a part of the night as the stars and the moonlight and as much a part of my life as anything else that ever was or ever will be.

There are many Loon Lakes. Canada has at least four Loon Lakes spread throughout four provinces. In the US alone, California, Illinois, Indiana, Michigan, Oregon and Washington each have a Loon Lake. Minnesota has *four* Loon Lakes, while Montana and New York each have two. One of those in New York is *my* Loon Lake. My particular Loon Lake is many different things, even just to me. As Twelve-Mile Creek is unremarkable as Lake Ontario tributaries go, so my Loon Lake is relatively unremarkable for an Adirondack Mountain Lake. Surrounded by cabins and fanning out in a wishbone shape, it's not very big, not very deep and not much more than a vacation destination except for a few year-round residents and many summer-home owners and renters. Once a year, usually in July, Joy and I are two of those renters. My personal history on Loon Lake goes much farther back, all the way to my very young childhood. My father grew up in the northern Adirondacks and our family vacations took place frequently at one cabin or another on the shores of Loon Lake. The vacations were often an extended-family affair with my cousins from the North Country and my paternal grandparents all spending time with us on the shores and waters of Loon Lake.

Some of my earliest fishing memories were of casting bobbers and worms around the creaky, splintery wooden docks. It seems in forty-odd years of retrospection that the lake provided an unlimited supply of willing bluegills and pumpkinseeds. In the evenings, Dad, my brother Alan, and I would join my grandfather for bullhead fishing by the light of the moon. Learning to skin bullhead with an old pair of needle-nose pliers is one of the finest memories I have of my Grandpa Spring.

There were always rowboats and canoes. Our family fishing trips often ventured out into the quiet mountain lake. There's a small, rocky island located nearly in the center of the lake. As a boy of about ten or eleven, I often awoke early and rowed out to beach the boat on the island and fish for the first few hours of daylight. Still years away from my driver's license, what freedom that boat represented to me! I'm not sure these days that parents would let their kids be quite so adventurous. I wouldn't let my kids row out there alone when they were ten, but times are different now. And now it's twenty-plus years since my kids were there. I don't see many lone kids out in their rowboats. That's a shame. Childhood freedom existed more commonly back then, resulting, I believe, in more independent and adventurous kids. Thanks Mom and Dad.

As a young adult, I took my own kids to Loon Lake on the

extended-family adventures. They grew up enjoying summer vacations playing with their grandparents, aunts, uncles and cousins. Rides around the lake with all of the kids squeezing in were often accomplished in my small outboard fishing boat or my brother-in-law Steve's bass boat. Sometimes the kids fished, but not as often as Steve and I. Whenever the kids were preoccupied or at least occupying each *other*, we would often head out in one of our boats to experience the northern pike and largemouth bass that often grew to surprising dimensions given the unremarkable nature of the lake. My fondest memories of those fishing trips were night-fishing ventures. I can't remember what year it was, but we discovered a gold mine of after-dark fishing. Using top-water lures we'd often entice very big pike and occasionally a nice bass. Much like my night fishing in the Catskills with Ken, it was as much a matter of feel and hearing as it was of sight. While gurgling a lure along the surface the splashy sound of a savage hit carried over the water. The reaction time, with no visual reference, was very often delayed and we found ourselves ducking Zara Spooks and Jitterbugs as they flew at us out of the darkness. The mosquitoes, drawn to the lights of the boat and the fish finder, were a constant menace, but the intensity of the night fishing proved more powerful than the painful welts we received. When a fish, usually a pike, wound up in the boat, lines frequently tangled and we found ourselves wrestling the beast in the dark with the hope of getting him unhooked without damage to any of the three of us. Although it didn't always work, I figured that the bloody puncture wounds from the treble hooks probably made for good chum.

Always, the call of the loons kept us company into the dark night.

There was a stretch of several years that Loon Lake was off my radar. With kids in high school and then college, I was busy working and writing. Somehow during that time, Loon Lake slipped away from me. Rather, *I* slipped away from Loon Lake. It was always there. Several years ago, Joy and I rented a cabin at Loon Lake and she, too, had its spell cast upon her. We haven't missed a year since.

In July 2016, Jennifer was in the last five months of her life. I wanted to cancel our vacation, planned long beforehand. But she wouldn't let me, and said she wanted to go with us. We knew the six-hour trip would be hard on her, but she was determined. Jen and her boyfriend, Matt, drove out separately, meeting us at the cabin. Jessica came along, as well.

Much like her day on Canadaigua Lake a month later, Jen was much diminished from surgery, chemotherapy and the advance of the cancer into the cognitive areas of her brain. She wasn't walking very well, wasn't remembering very well, and it was apparent almost as soon as she arrived at the cabin that this had not been a wise decision. The decision, however, was hers and I wasn't about to take it from her. Matt took her out for some boat rides in a small, blue rowboat that may well have been one of the same from the group of cabins just down the lake where we stayed when I was a kid. I'd like to think that it was the same rowboat I used to park on the tiny island. There's no way of knowing, of course. In my mind, though, it was.

The first afternoon, while Jessica, Joy and Matt talked on the beach, Jen and I sat on the short dock in the warmth of the afternoon. She looked out over the water, lost in thought. There was nothing I could do. I tortured myself, wondering what must be going through that highly intelligent brain. I still shudder to think of her thinking of her own death, but I'm sure that's what it was. How could it not be?

"Do you want to fish, kiddo?"

"No, that's okay. But why don't you fish and I'll watch."

She was so tired.

I'd leaned a rod rigged with a bobber and hook against the tree by the dock, in case she wanted to use it. Standing to grab it, I felt Jen's weary eyes on me.

"No spinnerbaits today, Dad?"

"Am I that predictable?"

"Yes, pretty much."

I laughed. "I thought you might just want some simple fishing, like when you were little."

"You mean when I was eighteen?" Her laughter was cackling and sincere, if a little quieter now.

I miss that cackle.

I rooted around in the yellow foam bait box and came up with a fat nightcrawler. Threading it on the hook, as I have a million times in my life, I tried one more time.

"Want to cast?"

"No, I'm good. I'm tired."

"I know you are."

A largemouth bass tugged the bobber underwater almost at our feet. It was surprisingly big. This time I didn't ask, but handed her the rod. She began reeling, smiling. I walked quickly to my kayak for the camera, but she stopped me.

"It's off, Dad. But thanks."

"Want to go inside?"

"Yes, please. I need to get some rest."

She slept a lot.

"Let's go."

"Did you think you were going to get a picture of me and my last fish?"

Her voice was quiet, and distant. She turned to me for the answer, probing me with her eyes.

"That's not what I thought at all. I've taken pictures of you and your fish since you were four."

She nodded as my heart broke in a thousand pieces. I'm surprised there were any pieces left to break. One thing I've learned in the months since she died is that there's no end to how many times your heart can break. That summer at Loon Lake, I'd only just seen the beginning.

Later, Jessica and Jennifer, Joy and I floated on tubes out in front of the cabin, lost in light conversation. Although we'd come to spend a lot of time together through Jen's illness, that is one of the last good memories I have of being with both of my daughters. Most of the memories of those last few weeks of togetherness are not good.

The next morning Jennifer and Matt left. When they got home, he sent me a text saying they made it all right, but Jen had been very confused on the way home. The trip had taken a lot out of her. She knew that Joy and I were staying a few more days, but repeatedly asked Matt if we were following behind them. I fished to keep myself busy at the cabin, a premonition of the year to come. Joy and I made a task of catching enough perch for dinner. Just at dark, the island where Mom let me fish when I was far too young gave us a couple of big walleyes. I didn't even realize there were walleyes in Loon Lake. Nice fish, but nothing could distract me from my anguish, my despair. I needed to get back to Jen. Not even the lifetime of memories or the soulful cry of the loons could console me until I returned home.

This year Joy and I returned to Loon Lake in July. The lake, though never bristling with activity, was especially quiet. Even on the night of the Fourth, very few of the lake's residents, permanent or otherwise, shot off the usual mix of cheap fireworks, always mildly entertaining after an evening of drinking wine on the beach by the fire. The loons, though, seemed to be all around. Even when I was a child, Loon Lake always lived up to its name and seldom failed to produce a loon. At the infrequent concussion of the sparse fireworks across the lake, the loons would answer, presumably in protest to the disturbance. Myself, I'd rather listen to loons. Lying awake at night under the open window, Joy and I marveled at their cries well into the night and on into the morning.

Even with the quiet kayaks, most loons don't allow a very close approach, diving out of the way and resurfacing a surprising distance away. However, on the second or third day, I spotted a strangely tame hen loon when we were bass fishing. Not wanting to harass the big bird, I nonetheless let my kayak glide within a few yards of it. Joy hung back, though the loon didn't seem to be distraught at our presence. A second loon—a smaller male—bobbed to the surface right next to her. Suddenly, the female's feathers ruffled and shuffled and two tiny heads poked out from beneath her wings. The male, carrying a small perch, swam up to the female and stuffed the perch down the closest young one's throat.

I paddled back to Joy and said, "I need to go get the good camera—now." She's pretty agreeable.

The paddle around the island and back to the cabin wasn't inconsiderable and by the time I snagged the camera and returned, we'd been paddling for a long time. The photography light was still good and I hung back with the camera, content to watch the loon family with the aid of the long lens. Not wishing to disturb the loons, we only photographed for twenty minutes or so, never approaching the birds directly. In that short time, the male brought no fewer than a dozen fish to the two young ones. At one point, they were using the female as a diving platform, leaping off her back and then climbing back up her tail feathers to repeat the adorable performance. We enjoyed watching them. When a slight gust of wind drove me too far across some imaginary loon boundary, the female let out an unusual cry and flipped her head back in what I can only assume was a warning. I felt bad.

We were done.

On the way back, I knew I'd gotten some of the best loon photos I've ever taken. I couldn't wait to load them onto the laptop and have a look. The first thing I thought was, *I need to send these to Jennifer.*

It's been almost a year and it still happens all the time.

Scary Monsters

O f all the days during my self-imposed exile on water, it was neither the slowest nor the best. In early July, the longnose gar were still very active on the surface of Oak Orchard Creek, basking in the mid-day sun and feeding heavily as the days drew on. The hour-long ride was worth it and the first three weeks in July saw me paddling the creek often more than once a week. The promise of multiple forty-inch predators was simply too much of a draw to me. I neglected my yard, my family duties and my other fishing pursuits. Three months into chasing them, I hadn't tired of sight fishing for those slimy dinosaurs.

One afternoon, I noted a dark shadow crossing the creek. I've seen some weird things in Oak Orchard, such as burbot and monstrous water snakes, but this was new. Paddling closer, I realized it was a massive school of emerald shiners. Shiners are basic prey items for everything from bass to bowfin, gar to salmon. I've often seen the creek teeming with them, but had never seen such a concentrated number. In the hot, mid-afternoon sun, they cast a massive shadow. A gentle ripple above them was the only disturbance they caused on the surface. I followed the school for several hundred yards. They met up with yet another massive school. The combined shiners numbered in the thousands. I took a few photos, but they didn't do the phenomenon justice.

Trying to locate gar, I left the school behind as I paddled slowly up the creek. A few minutes later, however, the water erupted behind me. I quickly paddled back down the stream and discovered the mayhem that had ensued in my absence. At least three large gar had begun slashing into the school of emerald shiners. One of them, an enormous female, was at the surface, her long and bony beak held high above the water before she slashed downward. The other two were just below the surface a few feet away. I watched the convulsive sideways swipes as they grabbed fish after fish after fish. The school of prey fish, once a nice round blob in the creek, did not scatter but rather stayed schooled and formed into a C-shape. The predators were attacking on the inside of the C and the shiners formed around them. Every now and then, an escaping minnow skipped across the surface, but mostly the group just held their position, presumably waiting for the onslaught to end. They didn't move away. Attracted to the carnage, seagulls whirled overhead and joined in the fray, diving into the living mass of fish. A half dozen gulls swooped in several times each, almost always successful in their diving runs, coming up with shiny two to three-inch shiners. Interesting as the lesson in natural history was, I focused on the largest of the three visible gar and dropped a rope-fly just past her nose when the time was right. Apparently fired up from the feeding frenzy, she didn't wait for the lure to pass her nose. Rather, she rushed it violently as soon as it hit the water. I paused and let her mouth it for just a few seconds and she was on. Tearing line off my spinning reel, she ran thirty yards out before I could turn her back toward the kayak. Once in the boat, she thrashed violently, probably annoyed that I had distracted her from the buffet. I held her up briefly for the camera, realizing that she was likely the biggest fish of the summer, well over forty-five inches. After another series of casts, I was able to pick up a small, spotted male as well. The two-footer was a bit of a letdown after the giant, but I was not disappointed as I let him go, realizing I'd already lost count of how many fish I caught over the course of the afternoon. That's a positive indicator of a pretty good day. This was icing on a slimy, ancient cake.

The gar activity slowed and I again paddled along the banks, slowly seeking out some more fish to target. An hour or so passed without a sighting so, more out of curiosity than anything else, I paddled back north in the direction of the big school of shiners. Maybe they'd attract some pike or something else. Lord knows, there's no shortage of scary predators in that creek.

I found not one but *two* concentrated pods of thousands of shiners. Each one made ripples on the calm surface and cast an ominous shadow. I approached the nearest school and eyed it carefully. It was a round, living mass of fish. Schooled very tightly, there was very little daylight between each shiner. I'm not sure I've ever seen anything quite like it. Later research would show such behavior is actually called *shoaling,* which is a bit different than *schooling.* Shoaling fish are frequently in that formation due to the presence of predators.

Of their presence, I had no doubt.

The sun began to sink lower in the western sky, casting the stream into shadow when the water again exploded. A small largemouth bass blew through the fish and into the air, mouth open. I slid the gar rod into its holder and quickly grabbed my spinnerbait bass rig. Before I could make a single cast, another and much larger bass also erupted to the surface, slashing through the baitfish and making multiple leaps. Yet another very *small* bass mimicked his larger cousins, also flipping above the school several times. It was a bass-on-minnow free-for-all. I was transfixed, but quickly snapped out of it when the rod in my hand reminded me I was also *fishing.*

Casting the spinnerbait into the living mass, I immediately hooked a very large largemouth. He tugged and fought. Several shiners skipped across the surface ahead of him but the larger school held together, forming once again into roughly a C-configuration. If anything, the school grew tighter during the chaos. Again, seagulls were instantly on-scene and slashing into the baitfish. This time, a nearby belted kingfisher also joined in, snatching several shiners out of the school to carry off and eat on a nearby branch. Usually the kingfishers are easily spooked, even by my small kayak. This one didn't have a care, eager to take part in the feast.

Later, paddling toward the launch after I'd boated two smaller bass out of the shoaling shiners in the glow of the setting sun, I reflected on the behavior I'd witnessed. I've always called Oak Orchard *Jurassic Creek,* but this was some pretty wild *Wild Kingdom* stuff for one afternoon. I couldn't help imagining what it must be like to be a part of that school.

It's hard to anthropomorphize something as alien as a small fish. They're not like us. Stretching my imagination a bit, though, I pictured what the human reaction would be to being simultaneously attacked by a bunch of scary monsters. Human behavior over the course of history would suggest all of the individuals in the human school would likely run for their lives, every person for themselves. Oh sure, there would be moments of heroism from a few select individuals, but we're pretty much programmed for *flight* rather than *fight*. I can't imagine a group of a thousand people quietly standing around while some big scary dinosaur ripped into them, eating several people in a gulp or two. The human mindset isn't cut out for the thoughts like "well, only some of us are going to be eaten…sit tight, it will be over soon." But that's precisely what was going on with those emerald shiners.

Remove the human behavior comparison and imagine the reality for a moment. You're one of those little two-inch fish. If you swim too close to the bank near a low-hanging branch, there's every likelihood you may be snatched from above by a water snake and swallowed alive. If you hang too close to the bottom, one of the hundreds of snapping turtles may snap you in half. You'd never see it coming. Or, how about the scenario I witnessed that July afternoon? You're swimming in a tight group, staying away from the banks, staying up off the bottom, and any number of predator fish (or even panfish) are taking turns swiping into your school, eating as many of you as it takes to get a bellyful. Perch, pike, bass, trout, salmon and burbot all have their turn at you. And then there are the dinosaurs—the gar and the bowfin that have fed on your ancestors since the dawn of time. They don't miss very often. Then, each time the surface is disturbed by one of these feeding extravaganzas, the seagulls and kingfishers are drawn to the area, commencing an air-assault on your already beleaguered school. You hang together more tightly and the group *tries* to avoid being eaten, but your only real defense is to hope someone else gets eaten, and not you.

I'm glad I'm not a fish.

Mr. G

Grief is a strange fishing partner. If Grief were a man, he'd have been uninvited from my fishing trips a very long time ago. I haven't uninvited many acquaintances, but he and I have spent far too much time together. His company has grown tiresome. With nothing to contribute to my outings but heartache, his familiarity has bred in me an especially virulent form of contempt. It's bad enough I have to deal with him at home and in my car, at work and pretty much everywhere else. Fishing has been my only escape from Grief, as imperfect as that escape can be some days. As November 2nd approaches, he seems to be a bit more insistent, a bit more melodramatic in his pleas for attention.

"Sorry…what? No, I think I'm just going to fish alone today, G. I'm hoping to catch some last-minute pike before the snow flies and I really need to concentrate. You do know I started this entire fishing campaign to distract myself from you in the first place, right? I think we need some space. A *lot of space.*"

"You wish. You wish," said G.

"Yes, I do wish."

"My feelings are hurt."

"Good. I'm glad they're hurt. Can you just stay away today, please?"

"You know I can't do that, though I can probably stay quiet for an hour or so if the fishing is good."

Knowing that would be the answer, I sighed. "Make it two hours and it's a deal."

"I don't deal."

"No, you don't."

"Where are we fishing? The tributary time machine?"

"Yes, G."

"And you want me to stay quiet? There? You make things hard some days, kid." He laughed. His laugh always sounds the same—the distant roar of a freight train carried on the cold north wind. I didn't respond. The phone went dead. G would like that phrase. He would laugh his cold freight train laugh.

Casting the pike lures into the increasingly chilly water at the mouth of the creek, I tried hard for some semblance of mindfulness. Instead of reaching out to the past or reaching forward into the future, I focused on the *now*. I tried, anyway. It's a technique I've never mastered. Still, I concentrated on the surging of the lure below the surface as I reeled in and tried to be aware of that exact moment. Focusing on the water a few feet behind the big jointed minnow, I watched for a follow. After an hour or so of mindful repetition, a small pike hit the lure. Only fourteen or fifteen inches long, he wasn't a whole lot larger than Randy's comical hot-dog pike on the day of "The Photo Shoot". How many months ago was that now? Time once again had a mind of its own.

Drifting upstream, back in time, without thinking about it, I eventually caught myself. I admired the pretty little pike that came to the boat for his chutzpah. He wasn't much bigger than the lure. The fish wasn't what I was hoping for, but when dropping him back into the water, I caught myself smiling. Smiles are a rare commodity these days, especially when I'm alone.

Suddenly, a tap on the shoulder brought me out of my mindfulness, or my fishfulness, anyway. I wasn't alone, after all.

"Kid?"

"Yes, G." The smile faded from my face.

"Has it been an hour yet?"

"Buy a watch. It's been two." There was no sense lying.

"That hurts, kid."

He wasted no time getting to work. The nightmare images came, eclipsing the day, eclipsing the moment, and eclipsing the precious now.

"I wish you would go away," I said through tears.

"I'm here for *you,* not for me. I don't even like fishing," said G.

"I'm not surprised."

"I know you hate me. Everyone hates me. You have your job and I have mine, so stop giving me…grief! Oh, that's a good one! I gotta write that down!"

"Yeah, that's a great one, G."

His deed completed for the afternoon, G vanished into the north wind, content. Boiling in a familiar cauldron of emotions, I returned to pike fishing, hoping for something bigger.

Hoping for something better.

Beneath the Surface

It is the dim haze of mystery that adds enhancement to pursuit.
—Antoine Rivarol

Two days after a festive yet unsuccessful return to salmon fishing, I was floating again on my kayak within the peaceful confines of the wooded banks of Twelve-Mile Creek. Note I didn't say *paddling alone* or *fishing alone*. I was just floating. I'd tried fishing in the heat of the late afternoon, but to no avail. Hoping to pick up on the beginning of the fall pike feeding frenzy, I had been casting large crankbaits and tossing white and chartreuse spinnerbaits in fast, rhythmic patterns. When it became apparent the fishing was just plain *bad* during the unusual heat wave of late September that was now moving into its second week, only by downsizing my offerings after the first hour did I hook a few small bass and a couple of nice perch. That was something anyway.

I hadn't planned on fishing at all. It was a lawn-mowing day and that was on my to-do list after work. Also on my to-do list was to water the flowers at my family plot in North Ridge Cemetery. I took the job over from my beloved, late grandmother, Mary Ruth. After Jen's interment in North Ridge, I took the solemn duty of caretaker even more solemnly. It came naturally, since I was up there almost every day and always at least twice a week since last November. A few family members and several friends told me it probably wasn't healthy to spend that much time among the dead, but the living weren't having much of me these days. Regardless, I was so used to seeing Jen every day after work, that, almost eleven months later, I couldn't break the habit; nor did I want to.

I can visit the cemetery with Joy or with Jessica and hold myself together reasonably well. There's always sniffles and tears, but I manage. When I go alone, I begin sobbing even before I drive through the front gates. By the time I reach the family plot, I am usually a mess. If I'm not, the last twenty steps from the driveway to my daughter's headstone unfailingly do me in. I've never considered myself cowardly, but neither am I particularly fearless. The inner strength to walk those few paces from the driveway to Jen's resting place requires more courage than I've ever had to summon over the course of my entire fifty years. It's *my child's headstone.* I hope you never have to cast your eyes upon such a thing. I wouldn't wish the feeling of approaching your kid's grave on my worst enemy. Never in a million years. It's a horror beyond horror and one that brings me to my knees—often quite literally—every time.

Though the Christian faith speaks warningly about communicating with the dead, I often talk to Jen at the cemetery, if only for my own good. I know she's not there. An angel might say, "Why do you seek the living among the dead?" But I haven't bumped into any lecturing angels and, though I hope beyond reason that Jen is enjoying life beyond our dimension, in our world she's most certainly absent, gone…dead. I won't tell you everything I say, but I always say that I'm sorry she was robbed of more time with us. The world needed more people like Jennifer Spring and it would take more than one heavenly being to stop me from telling her that. I always tell her I wish I could have protected her. To watch your child die feels like the ultimate failure as a parent and that sense of failure has enveloped every day of my life since November 2nd, 2016.

People see me at work, and they see me doing pretty much what I've always done. I see my friends, and I manage to have a laugh or two. None of them know the horror I'm experiencing every day. None of them know the anger and the bitterness. Nobody knows anything. Most days it stays below the surface and I can function. Other days it doesn't, and the sense of remorse and failure are front and center. Then, all I can do is disappear and try to keep myself busy.

I wished the fishing had been better.

Of all the horrors I experienced around Jen's death and now relive every day in mental images and almost every night in nightmares, a few weeks back a different piece of imagery came to me: Jen on a beach, smiling. I'm quite sure the image is from a photo I took of her many years ago on a beach in Virginia as a child, but in the mental image, it's the twenty-three year old Jennifer, smiling and healthy. I've only managed to conjure it a few times in the past months. It's very peaceful, and very comforting. I'm a visual creature and the images, both good and bad, have a profound influence on my state of mind. That image has been elusive, just below the surface, but when I am able to conjure it, it does tend to paper over the anger and sorrow at least for a few moments as I bask in its comforting glow. But an hour or so passed without a single cast as I sat and grew agitated on the calm water of my home creek, trying desperately to get the good image in my head.

Only the bad ones would come.

At dark, I looked at the paddle in my lap and considered going back up to the launch and then home. Instead I switched back to a large lure and began casting out into the creeping darkness. Hoping that the repetitive action of fishing would once again drive away the feelings of failure and despair, I cast as if my life depended on it. Maybe it does. A hundred or so casts later, nothing had come to the boat. Suddenly, off to the left side of my kayak, the water erupted. Two-inch emerald shiners jumped from the water as some unseen predator scattered them. A moment later, a deep wake raced across the surface as some larger fish again slashed into the baitfish. This time, another wake came in from another side and again the shiners went airborne. I watched closely as what appeared to be two large fish worked in tandem to herd the minnows into the center of the creek, not far from the old steel bridge. I'd seen gar do this teamwork thing before, but the very few gar I recently discovered were nowhere near this spot. Pike and pickerel tend to be solitary predators, as do bowfin. The mystery intrigued me as I waited for the next attack, hoping one of the predators would expose itself at least enough to give me a quick glimpse.

I stayed well past dark. Igniting my stern light, it was too dark now for any positive identification. I cast a few times in the direction of the oncoming hunters, but they ignored my offering, much more content with the feast of shiners. With the late mosquitoes turning on in earnest, attracted to my light, I decided to head for the launch. As I paddled away, I glanced briefly back several times and saw the hunt continuing in the growing moonlight. I wondered what they were. I like a mystery and this had captured my imagination, as most big fish do.

Distracted, my grief and anguish retreated to just below the surface again. I felt, at least momentarily, as if I could function again. I drove toward home, thinking about fish instead of failure.

It didn't last long.

An Early Fall

Crisp nights and the first crimson turning of the maples ushered in an early fall. Autumn's pen made shorthand notes on a precariously balanced summer far earlier than normal. It's the kind of fall I used to wish for. The vast majority of the writing I've done in my life has been about the magic of fall, and the ghosts of autumn. Hunting season has always kindled a warm fire in me that could beat away the coldest night. I can conjure up images of fall in my mind and on paper more easily than almost anything. It's how my brain has worked for a quarter of a century. This past year, though, I find myself hanging on to summer a little more tightly. I'm much less willing to let the warmth go and the cold take over. I would miss my fishing distraction, and I knew it. It's not as if I couldn't switch from fishing to hunting once the first snow spelled the end of fishing season. I could. But, as much as hunting has been a lifelong passion, I find myself less drawn to chasing game these days. Though there's still excitement enough in following Max, my golden retriever, through long fields of gold in search of pheasants—and I'll gladly shoot whatever he puts up—my heart isn't in it like it used to be. And deer season, which used to be the holiest of holies for me, wasn't the same last year after Jen died, and I'm quite sure won't be the same this year. I'll be out there, but not with the enthusiasm of previous years. I spent enough time in the company of death, and don't have any burning passion to be a *bringer* of death. Last year, I let several deer pass I could have shot. It was the first year I didn't shoot one in a long time. Maybe the passion will come back. Maybe this year I'll feel that burn again, but for now I just wanted to hang on to my fishing season and the relief and peace it has given me. Maybe it's just that the rhythmic casting and paddling of the fishing experience serves as a better distraction, keeping me busier than long hunting hours alone with my thoughts in the quiet woods. Until now, I haven't thought too hard about it, but fishing was pulling me harder than hunting. I was a fisherman long before I ever hunted and in some ways, I feel like I've returned to the headwaters of my life.

Not far from where we did "The Photo Shoot", the East Branch of Twelve-Mile Creek meets Lake Ontario. The East Branch is the big sister to the West Branch, my home water. The East Branch starts similarly to the origins of the West Branch, wandering down from the Niagara Escarpment and through farmers' fields. Unlike the West Branch, it widens into a broad harbor that is home to a yacht club, marina, a couple of good restaurants and an island of very nice homes. A large amount of the harbor shoreline is taken up with docks, pleasure boats, charter boats, and boathouses. The fishery is every bit as diverse as *my* branch. Many would say it's even better. Still, the steady boat traffic and lack of natural attributes make it, in my estimation, just not quite as interesting.

The wind blew in my face slightly from the northeast, far from ideal for fishing and for paddling. Once past the boat slips and summer homes, I paddled the deeper channel out to the piers. It quickly became apparent that the open lake was too rough for smallmouth fishing. However, where the west pier met the harbor, a tangle of willow trees, half submerged from the high water of the past months, looked like an inviting place to drop a lure. Maybe I'd come up with a largemouth or a pike. Word had it that this was a good pike spot.

The high gray clouds, looking not unlike snow clouds, seemed to be intensifying and rain wouldn't surprise me. Waiting for a pair of Canada geese and their mostly-grown goslings to move out of the way, I dropped a spinnerbait down into the branches. *Wham!* A big largemouth jumped to the air, thrashing and threatening to tangle us both in the willows. I hauled him in as quickly as I dared. I'm not a fan of heavy pound test, and at once wished I'd brought one of my very few rods I have rigged with it for just such locations. The bass was big, with dramatic lateral markings. Almost as soon as I'd gotten him into the kayak, the wind pushed me into the trees. I released the fish and silently cursed as I paddled backward out of the branches. Maybe it wasn't perfectly *silent* cursing, but I was aggravated to have drifted into such good cover. I didn't expect to hook another bass after disturbing their lair. Once safely back from the willow tangle, I cast again. The second cast produced a second bass, bigger than the first. It was easily a four-pounder and at first I thought it might be one of the open-lake smallmouths. It was another largemouth. Same pattern as last time: I fought the big fish as delicately as possible, trying to horse him out of the branches without breaking the line. I landed, photographed and released him all while drifting back into the willows.

Paddling backwards yet again, I watched warily as a large salmon charter came in between the piers. Obviously not too worried about the "no wake" signs, the captain was within fifty yards of me before he slowed the props. The initial wake from the fishing boat sent two-foot waves in my direction. The surge from the bow of the boat as it settled into the harbor sent a *four-foot* wave in my direction. The fishermen in the back of the boat watched with some concern as I rode the four-footer in my ten-foot kayak. The captain showed no such concern. Trying to keep my middle finger busy and out of trouble, I went back to casting as the cold rain began to fall.

In only a couple of dozen casts I boated eight big bass. There wasn't one less than three pounds and one that was a solid five. The rhythm was steady and I began to think of it as the *bass tree* instead of a willow. All eight bass came from within a few feet of each other. Watching my depth finder, I realized the branches were on the edge of the channel, providing the bass a perfect ambush spot for the shiners and shad coming in and out of the harbor. When the rain began, driven by the northeast breeze, I made a few more casts before turning back to the shelter of the creek. In the creek, I found no more luck. A little wet around the edges from the rain, I decided to call it a day—and a good one at that.

For the first time in many months, perhaps since March, I was chilled in a way that only autumn can chill you. I'm not sure I was ready for an early fall. It seems such a short time between the whites of winter, the browns of spring, the lush green of summer and the orange and gold of fall. These days, the colors seem to change so fast, as if they are all part of a quickly spinning kaleidoscope. I suppose that they are. Looking out over the lake, I breathed in the cool air. The pike should be feeding soon. The salmon would be running even sooner, if the early reports are correct. It's still calendar summer, but the ghosts of autumn are all around me. I guess it's not just autumn that's full of ghosts anymore. My whole life is full of them.

Across the channel is the bench near the pier where Joy's Uncle Jud spent many hours, talking with the pier anglers and getting the scoop on fishing conditions that he'd eagerly pass on to me during one of his many unannounced but welcomed visits. Visiting, dropping in, shooting the shit…call it what you will. It's a dying artform, and one at which he was experienced and adept. He was a master practitioner of shit shooting. Judson Myers always appreciated that he could drop in on us and frequently told us so. He was full of more fishing and hunting knowledge than anyone I've ever known. Jud was a part of the commercial fishing history of Lake Ontario. Now, that's ancient—almost alien—knowledge. Most people don't even know that there *was* commercial fishing on Lake Ontario. While Jen battled her brain cancer, Jud battled lung cancer. He frequently commented on life and death in large, simple terms I could understand.

"It's just not fair," he said to me after we buried Jennifer.

While not words of particular comfort, they at least rang true, then and now. True words are better than greeting-card platitudes.

Jud outlived Jennifer by seven months. His words of condolence made more sense to me than anything anyone else ever said. He repeated those words to me when he was dying as well. The bench by the pier is a much emptier place without him. Joy and I go there and sit now, sometimes together, sometimes not. As I paddled away from the bench and the cold, open water, the brisk wind blew, fooling August into thinking it was October.

It almost had me fooled, too.

Fishing Notes—June 1, 2013

Recollection is the only paradise from which we cannot be turned out.
—Jean Paul

*N*ow with a couple of kayak-fishing trips it's become undeniable that this is how Jennifer and I heal the rift in our relationship that has held its own since the divorce. Our third trip out it dawned on me how we were paralleling the healing course my dad and I took when we climbed the (Adirondack) High Peaks, seeking common ground. Like my time in the mountains with Dad, my fishing time with Jen doesn't consist of a lot of talk. What talk there is certainly isn't very deep. It's just a quiet repair of our relationship against the backdrop of some of the quiet backwaters. Common water instead of common ground. Nature seems to soothe us both in a way that puts us at peace with each other. It works for me, and I'm not surprised it's working for Jennifer, who's always been described as being so much like me, God help her.

Today's outing—trip number four—got Jen four fat largemouth bass and a very good blue heron photo. Nothing deep was exchanged in the course of conversation, but she just sent me a friend request on Facebook. A small step forward and a small admittance of me into her life. Jen was thrilled with the bass. (I need to have a talk with her, ha!)

Whatever's happening, I am glad.

The Return of the Kings

D uring most of the days documented in these pages, other than those dealing with fishing outings in my distant past, I've been a pretty miserable human being. In the wake of Jen's death, I find myself in that condition quite often. I hope I've detailed enough fun in these pages, however, to help you realize I'm not gloom and doom all the time. Most days, though, I'm gloom and doom with a side of silliness and hope, and hopefully that shows. If you're this far into the book, I'm assuming my melancholy moments weren't so oppressive as to cause you to throw yourself off a bridge. Thanks for staying here with me. I need the company. Besides, the only bridge around here is the bridge over Twelve-Mile Creek, and jumping off it would get you nothing except wet. A snapping turtle could bite you, I suppose.

For all my mixed emotions on the artificial Pacific salmon fishery (and the steelhead fishery to a lesser degree) in my home waters, it's hard to ignore the celebratory atmosphere when the king salmon return to the Great Lakes' tributaries. In years past, before snagging was outlawed, one particularly festive Niagara County destination was Burt Dam. These days, the Dam has become a bit of a punch line, due to the crowds, but it's still a spring and fall destination for anglers from all over the country; indeed, all over the world. Burt Dam is the choke point for Eighteen-Mile Creek, the big sister to my beloved Twelve-Mile Creek. A fly-fishing nerd from my teen years on, I used to fish Burt (as we locals call it) quite frequently. It's always overpopulated with fishermen once word gets out that the first trout or salmon have begun arriving at the dam. During the salmon snagging years, I'd still slog away with my fly rod, often landing huge salmon on small flies, while those around me were trying to stick a lead-weighted treble hook into their back. It was quite surreal fishing. Once someone—whether a real salmon fisherman or a snagger—hooked a fish, most of the other fishermen would pull their lines from the water so the lucky fellow (or accurate fellow, in the case of the snaggers) could land his fish without causing any major entanglements. They inevitably happened and I once saw an instance of a salmon crossing another salmon result in a fistfight. Now that's fishing!

The thing that stands out in my mind about the years I fished Burt Dam was the celebratory atmosphere. Oh, there were instances of crowding and the occasional exchange of harsh words when someone felt their territory was being intruded upon, but it was a festive atmosphere; especially so during the salmon run. The big salmon, splashingly obvious in the shallower gravel runs, were a source of great excitement. When snagging was outlawed (thankfully), the crowds remained and even grew. When I performed shift work, I'd often fish every morning in the spring and the fall. When I timed it just right and caught the beginning of one of the runs, I'd often only share the creek with a half-dozen other fishermen until word slowly spread or a story appeared in the local paper. With the instantaneous spread of information thanks to the Internet, there is no lag time now. Once the fish are in, so are the fishermen. It was around that time that I stopped fishing Burt, except as a place to take my out of town friends who just wanted to see and catch some big fish. Each time I played guide, I was more and more dismayed at the state of the crowded creek. Still, the atmosphere remained cheerful, even though being cheerful with so many people was difficult. I slowly adapted to fishing the smaller creeks, where I'm more at home. I'd rather catch fewer fish and deal with fewer people. I do miss Burt sometimes, though.

At the mouth of Twelve-Mile, Eighteen-Mile, and Oak Orchard Creeks are big double-piers. The piers, too, become one big party once the salmon arrive. As a teenager, I did a lot of pier fishing. It hasn't changed much since then. The fishermen run the gamut from inexperienced kids to weekend warriors, to seasoned pier-guys who have bags full of gear, chairs, and long-handled nets. As a kid, I remember it being a big deal when someone hooked up with a big trout or salmon. Much like in the creeks, the etiquette was such that everyone on that side of the pier would reel in to avoid a tangled mess of lines and fish. Most anglers complied. In the ensuing time as the lucky fisherman tangled with the fish, a crowd would form around the angler and watch as he battled the beast. If it looked like the fish would be landed (not at all a guarantee when it comes to a twenty-five pound salmon and an inexperienced fisherman), one of the more serious fisherman would jog down the pier with their gigantic, long handled net and subdue the fish for the lucky angler. The crowd usually remained long enough to admire the fish. A big king salmon is a sight to behold On the days that I was that lucky angler, the crowd reaction to a teenager was not unlike that for a rock star, if only for a few fleeting moments. Fifteen minutes of fishy fame.

The steady arrival and departures of the big salmon fishing charters always punctuated the festive pier activities. All summer long, they chug in and out of the harbors, but once the fish begin to stack up outside the mouth of the creeks, their frequency intensifies. When the salmon fishing is at its hottest, the boats come in at sunset, often lined up in the creek for their chance to dock, clean their salmon and take their photos. In the creeks, on the pier and out on the big water, the whole salmon run is a party.

I recently connected with an old high-school friend. I'll call him Dave because his name is Dave. An avid kayaker, Dave hadn't done much in the way of kayak fishing. He contacted me about the book, looking for some tips and local hotspots. I suggested gar fishing and was not surprised when he didn't join me. Those gar get no respect, I tell you that! Instead, he wanted to try salmon fishing. I don't know that a twenty-five pound king salmon is the way to gently ease yourself into the world of kayak-fishing, but I'm game for almost anything. Remembering Ken Reed's advice to never turn down a fishing invitation without a good excuse, I didn't need to think long about it. I poured through my gear, digging up some old salmon fishing lures, and bought a few new ones, agreeing to join him downstream of Burt Dam, near the mouth of Eighteen-Mile Creek. Reports of the fish beginning to pile up in the lower creek were coming in fast and furious, both in the news and on social media. I'd caught *almost* everything there is to catch from the kayak in my area, but had never hooked a salmon. I've battled enough of them from *real* boats and with the fly rod to know that I'd have my hands full if we managed to hook one. I joked with Dave as we made plans that if we *did* get into a big king, we may have to paddle back from Toronto, visible across the lake but some forty-two miles away.

I was excited in spite of myself.

Another friend contacted me with a hot tip about the fish piling up in a certain pool near the mouth of the creek. It would be our first stop. Arriving at the pool only a hundred yards from the piers and the lake, I was disappointed to find a small fishing boat anchored in the dead center of our destination. *Of course,* I thought. I hung back and watched the casting radius of the three fishermen and realized there was plenty of room to fish around the edges of the pool without disturbing them. The three young guys all waved and said hello. *That's a good sign.* As I was rigging up my huge Rapala (also from a hot tip), one of the boat fishermen hooked into a salmon. His excited cry of "*fish!*" echoed up and down the creek, reminding me of *fish!* from days gone by. The big salmon surfaced twice and I paused to watch. With only a minute or so on the line, he was off. The fisherman's shoulders slumped and his fishing partners began deriding him in earnest. I assume the fishing partners were also his friends, from the colorful language in use. Their laughter echoed up and down the creek.

I suddenly felt festive.

Dave, a hundred yards behind me, missed the action and I filled him in when he caught up. Getting his own gear rigged, he began casting against some boulders. I paddled around the fishing boat and to the opposite bank, so as not to crowd him. I'd keep an eye on him because I *desperately* wanted to see what would happen to an inexperienced kayak fisherman if he were suddenly to be towed by a king salmon—because he's my friend, *of course.*

Nearing the base of the west pier, I cast my impossibly large lure against the steel wall. My fishing pal who tipped me off to the west wall on the phone the previous night had landed an impressive twenty-five pound female here. I must say, I enjoy the challenge of getting a big fish in my small kayak, but I wondered what would happen. I could picture being dragged out between the piers and the pier fishermen yelling at me as I was towed through their fishing area. The thought was not inconceivable, though the pier people (from what I could hear) sounded quite festive themselves. Some may have been quite drunk as well. It's hard to say. If I hooked a king, I'd just hope for the best.

If not optimistic, I was at least excited.

One of my casts went a few feet too far and clanged sickeningly against the steel wall. I was sure I'd broken my lure. Suddenly, though, my offering was grabbed in a vicious sideswipe almost as soon as it hit the water. Picturing my friend's twenty-five pound fish, I reared back and set the hook as hard as I could. The fish pulled off a few feet of line as it headed for the bottom. I felt a few head shakes. Strike that, I felt a few *small* head shakes. If this was a salmon, it was certainly about twenty-four pounds short of a twenty-five pounder. Someone must have spotted me setting the hook, and a half-dozen people wandered down the pier to watch to see what might happen to an idiot who hooked a king salmon in his ten-foot bright green kayak. I probably would have done the same thing.

I reeled in slowly. There wasn't much of a fight. The largemouth bass popped out of the water between the gathering of pier fishermen and myself. Laughter ensued. Much of it was my own. I swear to you, I can catch bass when I am fishing for *anything*, but didn't expect one that afternoon. I'd set the hook so savagely, I'm surprised the bass survived it. I held him up for the pier guys to see.

"Bass on a J-13...now I've seen it all," the nearest guy said. I could hear him muttering to his wife as they walked away. I heard the word *kayak*. Not the first time. They laughed, at least. Another guy said, "Hey, it's something! You're doing better than I am!"

Festive.

I looked around for Dave to show him the fish, but he was still plugging away at the opposite side of the big creek. I released the bass— not a bad one at all, but not as impressive as a salmon—and went back to casting. On my very next cast—another pier-clanger—the lure was again snatched only an inch or so below the surface where it landed. I thought it must be the same bass. Maybe I'd brain-damaged him with my initial hook set. This time the line surged as my drag was peeled out. The fish headed toward the trio in the fishing boat and I yelled.

"Fish on!"

The boys in the boat began reeling in.

It wasn't a big salmon and I was able to turn it after two short runs. Reeling it close enough to the kayak to get at least a glimpse of it, I could see it was about a two-foot king salmon – and a skinny one at that. It suddenly recognized the kayak as a potential source of trouble, and zinged out line for a third run. I'd almost forgotten the power of these fish, even this relatively small specimen. The heavy bait-casting rod, slightly bent all this time, suddenly straightened and the line went slack. I thought he'd broken me off, and wouldn't have been surprised, but the lure was still there, still intact. I checked the line for nicks and cuts before I began casting again, repeating my *clang* method of bouncing it off the pier since it had resulted in two fish already. Dave paddled quietly up behind me. I told him the story as I cast toward the west pier, over and over, beating that rusty steel horse in hopes it would give up another fish. Bass, salmon, maybe I'd get a pike next. Who knows?

We spent the last hour of daylight out on the surprisingly calm open water of Lake Ontario just beyond the piers. The sun dipped low on the horizon and another beautiful Western New York sunset lit the glassy water with reds, yellows and gold. My entire life, I've never tired of these sunsets. Just before dark, salmon began jumping around us. I don't know why they do it. I'll research that and get back to you. But seeing a ten or twenty pound fish leaping from the calm water near the kayak is a sight to behold. I've often seen them do it in the creeks, too, also at sunset. They don't just *surface,* but rather *leap* from the water in a short arc, sometimes porpoising several feet in the air. It's very graceful. Each time one came out of the water nearby, I'd cast toward it hopefully, knowing there was at least a salmon in the vicinity. It's a big lake and you can't ignore opportunities like that.

The small sliver of sun above the horizon ushered in a stream of charter boats and, for safety's sake, we paddled back up into the creek away from the big boats and the encroaching darkness. The three young fishermen had vanished from the pool, replaced now by a young couple in kayaks.

"Doing any good?" Dave asked them.

"We are just fishing with worms. Got a few perch," the woman said, as if she needed to apologize for their preferred method of fishing.

After exchanging a little more fishing chat with the pair, Dave and I discussed future fishing plans in the growing darkness. A huge, hook-jawed male king salmon flew up in the air between us, diving back into the water with a surprisingly splashless entry. A perfect *ten* if I ever saw one. The woman cheered and laughed. Surprised at the proximity of the big fish, we both laughed as well.

It was nothing if not festive.

Yahrzeit

I'd spent the last few hours in the garage. For fishermen, preparation is a large portion of the fun. When I used to be an avid fly-tier, I'd spend many winter months at the desk, tying dozens upon dozens of flies in anticipation of spring. The activity filled in a void that couldn't be filled until the creeks thawed and the mayflies began again their mystical cycles of reproduction. Now, with my mind firmly on catching everything and anything in my kayak as a means of distraction, my off-time activities revolve around my garage workshop and my trailered kayak. I have racks in the garage where the other kayaks hang, but I like to keep my fishing kayak within easy reach. I can wander out into the garage and charge the fish-finder battery and shuffle tackle boxes about. Every now and then, I'll clean it up a little bit in a pointless attempt to restore it to its original beauty. It's the closest thing to working on cars that you'll ever find me doing. If you see my garage light on at night, I'm most likely working on the kayak.

My last pike fishing trip resulted in one perch, a bird's nest on a baitcasting reel and fouled line on one of my spinning rods due to my negligence in changing line (and you want me to change *oil?*). My third-string rod and reel combo got a hard workout that afternoon. So bad were my tangles, if I hadn't had the third rod I would have quit and gone home. Instead, I was able to pike fish as hard as I wanted to for the rest of the afternoon. The result? Bass. Bass, bass, more bass and another perch. While my fishing friends were proudly posting their fall bass on Facebook, I was channeling my inner Indiana Jones: *Why'd it have to be bass?* The pike were hard to come by this year.

After spooling fresh line on my two favorite heavy fishing rods (I might as well have just worked on my *bass* rods), I moved on to the tackle boxes. In the pre-season months, the condition of my kayak tackle boxes is a marvel of modern organization. Shiny new lures are sorted by color and type, sharing compartments with their closest cousins. Only a week into the season, however, the boxes were barely organized dumping grounds. Now, in the late season? Forget it. Retrieving a crankbait from one of them often means retrieving several in a long chain of treble hooks and brightly painted lures in all colors, sizes and types. It all goes to hell rather quickly. I decided I'd work on one of the smaller boxes. Besides, the season was almost over and I'd have all winter to dabble in such trivialities. When I finished one box, I moved on to another and another. It was ten o'clock on a work night, but I kept at it. With Joy sick on the couch, I needed the work to keep me company. It was one of those days, but worse. Also, it was too dark to go fishing.

October 2nd, if you do the math, is exactly a month from November 2nd. Trust me. Anyone in the process of grieving, especially the loss of a child, will tell you that anniversaries can have a profound impact on your psyche. It's not that the grieving process ever eases up, but those trigger-dates, especially big ones like the one-year mark, tend to focus the sadness, guilt and grief. I experienced it heavily on May 2nd and now, only one month away from the first year without Jen, I found myself almost in a panic, dreading that date. You may notice I didn't call it an anniversary. While trying to sort out my feelings and reading the words of other grieving parents, I've often come across the term *death-anniversary*. Anniversaries should be celebrations, and I refuse to use it. Just recently, I read an article suggesting the term *deathiversary*. Maybe it's just my current sensitivity, but I find the term ghastly. Do you buy a deathiversary cake? The word is morbid and I hope it's never widely adopted. A few weeks ago, I came across the Hebrew term *yahrzeit*. It's the Jewish period of mourning, particularly marking the years since death. Frankly, it just means year-of-death, which is no damned different than *death anniversary*. It is, however, at least to a Methodist boy, exotic and new. Yahrzeit beats deathiversary if only because it's foreign and not in my day to day vocabulary. I decided to adopt yahrzeit. I haven't had to explain it to anyone yet, because I only think of November 2nd as yahrzeit in my own head. There are yahrzeit candles in the Jewish tradition that are lit for twenty-four hours in honor of the dead. I like this idea. I suppose if I order the yahrzeit candles from Amazon, I'm going to have to sooner or later explain myself, if only for the fact they're adorned with the Star of David and Hebrew writing.

I hate having to explain myself.

Already, talk is buzzing about what everyone in my family is going to do on November 2nd. It's a Thursday and not easily tied into a long weekend. My first thought, of course, *was I want to go fishing.* I always want to go fishing these days. Of course, there will be time spent with our family, especially with Jessica, but I can fish well before anyone else is out of bed. I'm sure that's what I'll do. What else would I do? What else *could* I do? A few hours on the river of time thinking about my beloved and absent daughter would suit me just fine. I'm sure I can catch a bass or two.

Still sorting through my messy tackle, I took the box over and sat on the big, comfortable lawnmower seat next to my kayak. I thought about how cold November 2nd would be out on the water. Probably *too* cold, but I thought that's where I would need to be.

Cold comfort.

I finished a third tackle box and thought, *what the hell,* moving the rest of them to the hood of the lawnmower as well. I was on a roll. Tomorrow afternoon would be another pike fishing trip. I wondered how big the bass would be this time. The day after that, I'd be at Eighteen-Mile Creek trying for salmon. I really didn't want to salmon fish all that much, but when my friend, Dave (we're calling him *Dave* if you recall), caught a big one in his kayak, I was moved into action. It's important I stay ahead of him in accomplishments so he can remain my fishing partner. I had a few more off-days during which I could get some last-minute fishing in. I wanted to fill the days from now until the end of the month with fishing. The busier I stayed, the less I would focus on and dread November 2nd.

Yahrzeit.

Digging through the shelves next to the kayak, I found more gear that I could organize, whether it needed it or not.

Time, Stand Still

It is only in appearance that time is a river. It is rather a
vast landscape and it is the eye of the beholder that moves.
—*Thornton Wilder*

If Twelve-Mile Creek represents my life's timeline, it may be noteworthy finding myself spending much of my time at the end these days, at the mouth of the creek. It's not symbolic. I don't feel like I'm at the end of my timeline. I hope not, anyway. I'd fish farther upstream in some of the old familiar pools, but they're not accessible. Not right now anyway. The duckweed that started choking off the creek weeks ago has become a solid mat. The upper reaches likely won't be open now until next spring. In the intervening months, my creek will be socked in with ice, marked only by the occasional snowmobile track or ice-fishing hole drilled by some cold, lonely fisherman. There's no paddling back upstream to my past. The time machine is temporarily out of service, for now anyway.

Maybe that's a good thing. I don't know.

Drifting near the mouth, casting large crankbaits for what I hope will be either a salmon or pike, I have a secret.

It's a good one.

Jessica is carrying her first child and our first grandchild. She has an app on her phone that tells her each day about that day's stage of development and its size. We've called it variously *grandgrape, grandpecan and (my favorite) grandkidneybean.* She's telling the family next week. The heartbeat is strong and the baby looks perfect. For now, though, it's still a secret and Jessica is bursting to tell. It will be the first new baby in the family in many, many years. The happiness of that anticipation is a wonderful and welcomed change for me.

I'm excited and happy for my daughter and CJ, but I can't help carrying with me a small sense of apprehension. After the loss of Jennifer and the heartache our entire family has endured for the last couple of years, I feel a lot of responsibility will be placed on this little baby. Jessica's child will become the focus of everyone's attention for a very long time. It will have the burden of being the bright beacon of hope and happiness in the colorless bleakness we've struggled through since Jennifer first got sick.

That's a lot to ask of a grandkidneybean.

Still, to be the object of so much love and hope is how *every* child should come into this world, isn't it? I've found myself praying again. Mostly, I am giving thanks but at the same time asking God not to screw this up. A non-traditional prayer to be sure, but I think He understands.

Fishing season is almost over. A few more weeks and I'll have to clean the kayak and put it up for the winter as the lake conditions become too cold and dangerous for my taste. Maybe I'll start hunting soon. I have a six-year old Golden Retriever who didn't have much of a pheasant season last year. Max deserves some birds even if my heart isn't in it.

My exile, my self-imposed isolation while fishing for the meaning of life, is nearly over. Quiet meditations on death in my home creek have taken me as far as they will, for now anyway. I need to find something to do with the cold months until fishing comes around again. I'm going to require another distraction. Fishing may not take such precedence next year, though, with the new baby arriving in May. While fishing and paddling have been a mostly positive distraction, Jessica's news has been an unassailable ray of hope in the eclipse.

We needed that.

For a moment, content *in* that moment, I looked neither back to the agony of the recent past or hope for the future. I just enjoyed the secret knowledge of that little baby and all it represented *right now.* For a moment, I was able to make time stand still. It's a skill I wished I had honed before Jennifer left us. Maybe that moment was another gift from Jen.

Just be, Dad.

Casting at the base of some trees near the mouth of the creek, I hooked a largemouth bass. Of course I did. A very nice bass, and if it were the last fish of the year it would have been a respectable way to celebrate the end of the season. It wasn't the last fish, though. At the time I had no way of knowing a warm front was soon going to usher in fourteen days of autumn warmth and I'd be fishing long past the time I should have started bird hunting. That's okay. I'm glad I didn't know. It may have ruined the moment—the *now.* Soon enough the nights would grow colder, the leaves would turn to gold and blanket the surface of my little creek as it began its winter's rest. *Soon enough.*

In her short life Jennifer the Lion-Hearted *lived.* The only way I can honor her is to move forward, seeing the beautiful things and experiencing the life that she no longer can. I've no intention of moving *past* the grief over my daughter. There's no way I could, but I will keep moving. There's a half-completed painting she started for me when she first got sick. It's two people in a canoe on a small lake. It looks an awful lot like Harwood Lake. That unfinished artwork is as powerful a message as any Jen ever gave me.

Ahead of me, Lake Ontario sprawled, the Toronto skyline a distant mirage on the other side of the lake. The day's waves lulled themselves into a quiet sleep as the sun slipped low in the sky. I paddled out onto the open water. It wasn't the end of my creek, but the beginning of something else.

Acknowledgements

This book is a river with many sources, fed by many springs and many Springs.

Jessica Taylor, my oldest daughter, who held herself so gracefully during the darkest period of our lives, has provided me with smiles and inspiration since the day she was born. From the day her little sister was born until the morning she died, Jessica took care of her as a third parent. I have never been more proud of Jessica. Communicating with her through every day of the last several years has been an island of sanity in great lake of torment. The world needed more people like Jennifer Spring, but the world *needs* more kind, thoughtful people like Jessica Taylor. She gives me hope for the future. Jessica is a blessing to all around her.

Joy Spring signed onto this marriage as we all do, probably not knowing what she was getting into. Over the last few years, Joy has carried me through our living nightmare and back out the other side. I have often been a heavy burden to bear but she never once stumbled. I've fallen many times and Joy is always there either to pick me up or to encourage me to pick myself up. I couldn't have asked for a better partner with whom to traverse the darkness of last few years. I'm not sure I would have made it without her. Her encouragement, as always, was a driving force in seeing these sometimes difficult pages come to life. Joy has always been my rock in the river of time.

My parents, Marvin & Jayne Spring, not only introduced me to Loon Lake, a place of family and healing, but also have provided encouragement throughout my life. Through every day of Jennifer's battle, they were the best grandparents my daughter could have ever hoped for. Thanks Mom & Dad.

Many thanks belong to Bill Hilts, Jr. and Jerry Kustich for believing in this book and for the endless months of thoughtful encouragement, suggestions, and friendship. Thanks guys.

For sharp-eyed music aficionados, you may have noticed several chapter titles in *Strong is the Current* are song titles. "On an Island" and "A Boat Lies Waiting" are David Gilmour songs. "A Boat Lies Waiting" is especially poignant to me and to the story that bears its name. Another song that is not a chapter title but is mentioned within the text is "Just Be" by Styx. It's an apt summary for the serenity I sought during those lonely months on the water. Finally, the song that sums up what I was attempting to say in this book is "Time Stand Still" by Rush. Each morning for months after Jen's death, I played "Time Stand Still" in my truck while badly singing along. It was my war cry. Each day I heard something new in that song that pushed me towards writing the words you've just finished reading.

About the Author

A native of Western New York, Joel Spring is the author of *The Ghosts of Autumn, The Ultimate Guide to Kayak Fishing, Season of Obsession, Thursday's Bird* and many sporting magazine articles. Joel makes his home in the small town of Ransomville, NY with his wife, Joy.